Nationalism— Friend or Foe of Liberalism?

EDITED BY
Brian Tierney,
Donald Kagan &
L. Pearce Williams
CORNELL UNIVERSITY

RANDOM HOUSE HISTORICAL ISSUES SERIES 17

$.95

Nationalism

Random House Historical Issues Series

GENERAL EDITORS:

BRIAN TIERNEY

DONALD KAGAN

L. PEARCE WILLIAMS

CONSULTING EDITOR:

Eugene Rice

NATIONALISM—
FRIEND OR FOE
OF LIBERALISM?

Random House

Preface

A major purpose of this series of pamphlets is to convince students in Western civilization courses that the essential task of a historian is not to collect dead facts but to confront live issues. The issues are alive because they arise out of the tensions that men have to face in every generation—tensions between freedom and authority, between reason and faith, between human free will and all the impersonal circumstances that help to shape our lives.

In order to achieve any sophisticated understanding of such matters, a student needs to read the views of great modern historians as they are set out in their own words. He needs to develop a measure of critical historical insight by comparing these often conflicting views with the source material on which they are based. He needs above all to concern himself with the great issues that have shaped the course of Western civilization and not with historical "problems" that are mere artificially contrived conundrums.

We believe that there are three major themes whose development and interplay have shaped the distinctive characteristics that set Western civilization apart from the other great historic cultures. They are the growth of a tradition of rational scientific inquiry, the persistence of a tension between Judaeo-Christian religious ideals and social realities, the emergence of constitutional forms of government. These three themes are introduced in the first pamphlets of the series. The reader will find them recurring in new forms and changing contexts throughout the rest of the pamphlets. We hope that in studying them he will come to a richer understanding of the heritage of Western civilization—and of the historian's approach to it.

Ithaca, 1968   BRIAN TIERNEY

DONALD KAGAN

L. PEARCE WILLIAMS

Nationalism—Friend or Foe of Liberalism?

CONTENTS

QUESTIONS FOR STUDY

1   *What does Snyder feel are the essential elements of nationalism? To what extent would Fichte agree with him?*

2   *What did Fichte think were the essential elements of German nationalism? Who would he consider a German?*

3   *In what ways do Schurz and Baumgarten differ as examples of German liberals?*

4   *Was it inevitable that liberalism and nationalism come into conflict in Germany?*

It could be argued that nationalism has always been with us. Pro patria mori (to die for one's country) was considered the highest good in ancient Rome, and the cry, "God acts through France," echoed through the Middle Ages. But these manifestations of nationalism were sporadic and submerged beneath strong feelings of local custom and tradition. It was the French Revolution that created the upsurge of national feeling that was to swell and grow throughout the nineteenth century until the principle of national self-determination was recognized as a natural right in the twentieth. The French Revolution also gave great impetus to liberalism, to the idea that men have natural rights and that the purpose of the state is to guarantee them. One of the great questions of the nineteenth century was what to do when there was, as yet, no national state that could effectively guarantee the rights of man. Was it not obvious that the state must first be created if rights were to have any meaning? Or was it enough to struggle for rights in the hopes that the small principality would be too weak to suppress them? But what then of one's stronger neighbors? Who would protect the citizen's rights if, as during the Napoleonic wars, the state fell to an invader? These questions were basic to the evolution of the German state in the nineteenth century, and it is the conflict among some of them that forms the basis of this problem.

1 The Nature of Nationalism

Nationalism is not a simple idea to define. It is a whole constellation of philosophical and emotional factors that combine to create a feeling of being a part of a national group. The dimensions of this feeling, as it applies to Germany, are described by Professor Snyder of the City College of New York.

FROM *German Nationalism* BY LOUIS L. SNYDER

THERE IS GENERAL AGREEMENT among historians on the existence of nationalism as an idea of enormous significance that has penetrated into every phase of modern life. The attitude which ascribes to national individuality a high place in the hierarchy of values is not only an idea in the Platonic sense, but a reality which is of great importance in the study of history. On the corollary of "national character," however, there is a strong, often bitter, difference of opinion. Three points of view may be noted: (1) there is no such thing as "national character"; (2) "national character" is a demonstrable historical idea produced by variable social influences, and it remains constant among a people from first to last; and (3) the persuasion that certain types of character belong to certain people in certain areas has a limited validity if it intends to convey the idea that certain values have been inculcated within cultures by responses to different calls from without—by traditions, by ethical institutions, and by education. The first two points of view represent extremist thinking on the problem, while the third recognizes the existence of national character without minimizing the difficulties faced in determining its meaning and nature.

Until recently the idea of national character was regarded by respectable social scientists as only a metaphysical dream shot through with fallacious generalizations and unreflecting prejudice. With a little ingenuity and sophistry, it was said, it is possible to deduce two entirely different sets of characteristics for any nation. The contention that each nation has a char-

Louis L. Snyder, *German Nationalism: The Tragedy of a People* (1952), pp. 1–5, 7–12, 16–20. Reprinted by permission of The Stackpole Company.

acter of its own, it was further claimed, is mere superstition, and so-called national differences can be fully accounted for by the undeniable characteristics of individual psychology.

The second point of view, which goes to the opposite extreme, was expressed by Henry Morley in the statement that "in the literature of any people we perceive under all contrasts of form produced by variable social influences the one national character from first to last." The idea of a fundamental national character, a concept borrowed from Montesquieu by some German writers, notably Herder, in the late eighteenth century, developed in the nineteenth century into a persuasion that national characters existed which helped to mould the destiny of nations. This school had so much faith in fixed national character that it gave the concept an important place as a prime moulder of political, social, and economic institutions. The procedure was to prove that the *Volksgeist* (people's spirit), the *Volksstimme* (people's voice), and the *Volksseele* (people's soul), were compounded of certain desirable characteristics which showed the superiority of one people over another. By the same token, other peoples were regarded as inferior national groups. Emphasis was placed upon such externals as language, dress, and social habits. From this school believing in a permanent, stable national character arose such stereotypes as the realistic and volatile Frenchman, the emotional and cynical Italian, the phlegmatic and self-assured Englishman, the frugal Scotsman, and the aggressive and naïve American. These sweeping generalizations have little scientific validity without careful frequency analysis, but they have persisted as popular beliefs.

The third position, and the one we shall accept here, recognizes the limited validity of the idea of national character, but does not reject it for that reason. It is aware of the difficulties encountered both in defining national character and in measuring its quality. The term has validity only if it is intended to convey the idea that within certain cultures distinct values have been inculcated by environmental conditions, historical institutions, and formal education. It is intended to show that different aspects of the complex character of man respond to different environmental conditions, and that separate groups, as well as individuals, react socially in diverse ways. From this point of view it is unwise to reject altogether the psychological differences among nations in favor of the more impersonal factors of economics and military power.

It will be noted that nothing has been said in this position about national character as if it were something biologically inherited. Much of the confusion that has existed in treating this problem in the past has been due to the common practice of confusing the term with the obscure designation "racial character." Since racialism has been exposed as a meaningless fraud, few historians now speak of national character as if it were inheritable. It is obvious that national character could not possibly consist of such inherited characteristics as are organic and inborn. Because of this confusion of meaning, many historians tend to shy away completely from the term "national character," on the assumption that, no matter how carefully they distinguish between nationalism and racialism, they will be accused of subjective thinking and propaganda.

It is useless to insist upon a rigid constancy of national character. Throughout history there have been frequent characterizations of common attitudes and traits of peoples, some of which persist for a long time and others of which apparently change under the influence of historical developments. It is possible that an important transformation can take place in the character traits of a people. The French of the early eighteenth century were generally considered to be a stolid, peace-loving people, yet, within a century, they had undergone a violent revolution and were attempting to impress their ideas upon the rest of Europe by means of Napoleon's sword. Similarly, the once impractical, comfortable Germans of the Holy Roman Empire and the Confederation, petty and bourgeois in their ideas, emerged into a leading position in industry and business in the late nineteenth century, and, proud, hard, and arrogant, found themselves involved in two world wars. The English, once regarded as a people inclined to revolution, are today considered to be one of the most stolid and stable people on earth. Clearly, then, the notion of a *permanent* national character cannot be sustained.

That there is at least a *relative* uniformity of national character is an entirely different matter. Indeed, some national traits show an extraordinary persistence and power of survival. Each individual is exposed to those forces which make up the idea of nationalism—common history, common institutions, common historical traditions, common historical heroes, and, perhaps, common language, literature, and religion. The individual tends to identify himself with the predominant group of the age in which he lives; in other words, he treats the events that happen to the group as though they happened to him, as if the body of society were his own body. This process of identification, partly sensible and objective, and partly imaginative and false, accounts for the obvious intensity of group life. The individual may or may not absorb all the qualities of the national character, especially since in modern, complex, industrialized societies the factors conditioning character may be involved or contradictory. Nor does it necessarily follow that the national character will be the sum total of the individuals' characters, as there may be extraneous factors existing over which the individual has little or no control. The majority of people in a given country may abhor the idea of war; nevertheless, they find themselves part of an aggressive people bent upon seeking for themselves "a place in the sun." The national character may be at variance with the personality of the individual member of the nation, as there are always large numbers in any society who fail to conform to type. It is possible that even a conforming individual may act atypically on occasion.

*   *   *

The role of the historian in the new study of national character stems from the fact that institutions often reflect mainly the influence of dominant groups, hence "analysis of a nation's current institutions must be supplemented by historical and causal studies." The course of German history has shown that there is a conspicuous lack of balance in the national character. The duality of German conduct is a striking phenomenon. German greatness of purpose and achievement have often been combined with a vague, romantic foolhardiness. The Germans may be sentimental and good-hearted and at the same time unpredictable and dangerous. The tradition of internal quarreling made the Germans either frivolous or ruthless, or else they took refuge in philosophy and mysticism because the world seemed to be too harsh for them. The number of eccentric types in Germany is inordinately large. Harmony in the Germans is rare.

The outstanding fact of German history is a polarity of development and a dichotomy of ideas and procedures that has never been resolved. The history of the Germans has been the history of the unending struggle between the continental Teutons for a working compromise between uniformity and disruption. Uniformity was, and is, contrary to the ethnic, political, and cultural divergences of the Germans. At no time in German history has there been one central power strong enough to crush the centrifugal tendencies of the component parts. At no time were the individual parts weak enough to allow themselves to be merged into one highly centralized body, with the exception of the short-lived Hitler Reich.

*   *   *

. . . The idea of the independent unit was an early theme in German history. Both Caesar and Tacitus testified to the fierce sense of independence of the early Germanic barbarians. German feudalism in the Middle Ages was torn by disintegration.

Superimposed on this dualism of centralism versus particularism was an even greater dichotomy—the conflict between national unity and theocratical world monarchy. While England and France emerged in early modern times as national states, in the Germanies there was a fruitless pursuit of idealistic dreams of a theocratical world monarchy.

*   *   *

The persistent dichotomy appeared again in the struggle between Austria and Prussia for domination of Germany. The Austrian monarchy controlled a consolidated territory that extended from the Swiss-Tyrolean border to the Polish frontier. Starting as a product of German particularism, Prussia expanded on eastern colonial ground, and, by the time of the reign of Frederick the Great, had arisen to a place of importance in Europe. The dualism between Austria and Prussia continued through the first half of the nineteenth century. After the Congress of Vienna in 1815, the Metternichian policy or domination was imposed on Prussia until Metternich's collapse in 1848. The professors of the Frankfort Assembly had a golden opportunity to create once and for all time the hotly desired German unity, but these well-meaning men found themselves on the horns of a dilemma. Was there to be a "Big German" (*grossdeutsch*) solution, which would include the Germans of Austria, or a "Little German" (*kleindeutsch*) settlement, which would leave out the Austrian Germans? German liberalism was to be submerged in the frustrations of this dualism.

Once German unity had been fashioned in the crucible of Bismarck's wars, and once the German Empire of William II felt itself ready for expansion, it might have been expected that the tragic dichotomy would be resolved. But not so. This time Germany was caught between East (*Drang nach Osten*) and West. The Empire created by Bismarck in 1871 sought a solution in a kind of half-hearted combination between Western constitutionalism and Eastern authoritarianism. Prussia, the state of soldiers and officials, was the determining force in the government, and the voice of the people was heard but faintly in the *Reichstag,* an ineffectual debating society. The German Emperor, who was at the same time King of Prussia, exercised semi-autocratic powers through his Prussian office.

✳   ✳   ✳

There is a strong historical reason for the curious German predilection for philosophic systems, abstract ideas, and cosmopolitan dreams. With little opportunity to take part in practical political affairs, the Germans sought to exercise their minds in intellectual contemplation, as indicated by the enormous popularity of philosophy in nineteenth-century Germany. Following the lead of Kant, German philosophers, such as Hegel, Schelling, Fichte, and others, and the historical school of law and politics, such as Savigny, Adam Müller, Friedrich Stahl, and others, sought to give ideas and ideals a predominant position in the scale of human values and to convert them into an exclusive pillar of the universe. Hegel, especially, made liberty the pivot of political philosophy, but withdrew this liberty from the individual and transferred it to the State, thus bringing about a union between idealism and absolutism. Unlike the earlier philosophers, the Germans took, not man, but *German man* as their primary concern, thus making the objective of the mind, which in Europe generally had been considered the universal good, the particular good of German nationalism. Treitschke expressed this trend in a revealing passage: "Depth of thought, idealism, cosmopolitan views; a transcendental philosophy which boldly oversteps (or freely looks over) the separate barriers of finite existence; familiarity with every thought and feeling, the desire to traverse the worldwide realm of ideas in common with the foremost intellects of all nations and all times—all that has at all times been held to be characteristic of the Germans and has always been praised as the privilege of German character and breeding." This preference for philosophic systems, accompanied by a self-righteous rejection of the actual forces at work in the world, resulted in a dangerous political immaturity.

The end result of this predisposition toward philosophical abstractions was a gradual shifting to a mythological attitude which was, in effect, a battle against the temper of Western civilization. Aurel Kolnai described this defiance of reason and morals in a significant passage:

> This self-conscious subjectivism, this deliberate sacrifice of the intellect, this methodological training to barbarian *naïveté* has an almost touching air of heroic perversity about it. What is its meaning? Apart from the general "weariness of civilization" and the historical antagonism to the nations and forces that represent it, roused to fever-pitch by the War and its sequel, the Call for Mythology is also in line with the political conception of the Totalitarian Tribe and the anthropological and religious conception of the Master Man, the Superior Race, the Sacred We. Objective Truth, enduring and detached (be it of the religious or the scientific order), portends deadly injury to the triple identity of Tribal Egotism: the identification of the racial Self, the Master Set, and Deity. . . . In brief, the call for mythology indicates the will to break the spiritual backbone of man, to supersede personality, with its consciousness of eternal relations, by a flabby vital stock of ethnic purity, to pull down the last strongholds of the mind in which human freedom and dignity could entrench themselves against the totalitarian encroachment of an insane and godless tyranny.

The point of view expressed by L. B. Namier, Professor of Modern History in the University of Manchester, England, is one for which the remainder of this book will attempt to present historical evidence in various fields:

> Most types of social groups can be found, in one form or another, in all nations, but attaining various degrees of development and importance; and some nations develop into one or two forms into dominant patterns which express national character and their communal life. Thus the pattern forms of England are Parliament and the team, of Germany the State and the army, or perhaps rather the army and the State. Characteristic of the English social groups is the degree of freedom which they leave to the individual and the basic equality of their members, the voluntary submission to the rules of "the game" and the curious mixture of elasticity and rigidity in these rules; most of all, the moral standards which these groups enforce or to which they aspire.
> Characteristic of the German social groups is the utter, conscious, subordination of the individual, the iron discipline which they enforce, the high degree of organization and efficiency which they attain, and their resultant inhumanity. The State is an aim in itself, while that of

the army is essentially a-moral—to smash the enemy. Whatever characteristics in the individual members of the two nations have gone to form
these patterns, and whatever share circumstances had in their development, once crystallized these patterns powerfully react on the individual
and mould him in turn. Removed from this setting the individual may
develop, or at least seem to develop, in a different manner: still, it is the
pattern which expresses the national character.

The contention that national extremism was a bolt out of the heavens, a
"catastrophe" that suddenly appeared to plague the German people, is inac-
curate and untenable. German extremism did not occur in a vacuum; its
roots lay deep in German history for the last century and a half. Behind it
was a pattern of thinking tempered by nationalism, romanticism, and histori-
cism. The Germans who were shocked and amazed by the excesses of
Hitlerism never understood that the political régime which almost led them
to national destruction was the logical outcome of a long and dangerous
intellectual tradition.

*   *   *

It would be incorrect to assume that the line leading to German integral
nationalism was absolutely clear and unchallenged as it ran through the
course of the nineteenth century. The golden age of German universalism,
epitomized in the thinking and works of Lessing, Humboldt, Goethe, Schiller, Beethoven, and Mozart, ended in the frustrations of the nineteenth
century as the Germans apparently became exhausted by their sudden and
dizzy ascent to politico-economic power. But even in that century, in which
the German character was moulded in the Prussian tradition, there were
some thinkers who were appalled and disgusted with the rapidly accelerat-
ing extremism. Heine and even Nietzsche ("nationalism is disease and
madness") heaped ridicule on German provincialism and urged their fel-
low-countrymen to mature into citizens of the world. As other countries,
Prusso-Germany had a supply of liberals, rationalists, socialists, international-
ists, cosmopolitans, and pacifists, but they were always a relatively small and
isolated group with voices crying in the wilderness. Their ineffectiveness
testifies to the strength of the culture-power advocates who moulded the
German mind in their own image. The masses were so politically inarticu-
late and immature that even socialism, which was supposed to stem from the
yearnings of the lower classes, received its stamp from above and became
"Prussian socialism" and "national socialism."

Our procedure will be to select representatives of various fields and show
what they contributed to the rise of extremist thinking in Germany. Several
advocates of German liberalism are included to demonstrate the weakness of
the liberal position contra extremism.

2 Liberalism and Nationalism in Post-Napoleonic Germany

In 1806 Napoleon's army crushed the Prussians at Jena, and Prussia found herself, for the first time, a subject nation. It was in answer to the despair that gripped the Fatherland that Johann Gottlieb Fichte (1762–1814) gave a series of addresses intended to reveal the uniqueness of the German nation and its historical destiny.

FROM *Address to the German Nation* BY J. G. FICHTE

I SPEAK FOR GERMANS SIMPLY, of Germans simply, not recognizing, but setting aside completely and rejecting, all the dissociating distinctions which for centuries unhappy events have caused in this single nation. You, gentlemen, are indeed to my outward eye the first and immediate representatives who bring before my mind the beloved national characteristics, and are the visible spark at which the flame of my address is kindled. But my spirit gathers round it the educated part of the whole German nation, from all the lands in which they are scattered. It thinks of and considers our common position and relations; it longs that part of the living force, with which these addresses may chance to grip you, may also remain in and breathe from the dumb printed page which alone will come to the eyes of the absent, and may in all places kindle German hearts to decision and action. Only of Germans and simply for Germans, I said. In due course we shall show that any other mark of unity or any other national bond either never had truth and meaning or, if it had, that owing to our present position these bonds of union have been destroyed and torn from us and can never recur; it is only by means of the common characteristic of being German that we can avert the downfall of our nation which is threatened by its fusion with

Johann Gottlieb Fichte, *Addresses to the German Nation* (1922), pp. 3–4, 206–9, 227–33, 235–6, translated by R. F. Jones and G. H. Turnbull. Reprinted by permission of The Open Court Publishing Company, La Salle, Illinois.

foreign peoples, and win back again an individuality that is self-supporting and quite incapable of any dependence upon others. With our perception of the truth of this statement its apparent conflict (feared now, perhaps, by many) with other duties and with matters that are considered sacred will completely vanish.

Therefore, as I speak only of Germans in general, I shall proclaim that many things concern us which do not apply in the first instance to those assembled here, just as I shall pronounce as the concern of all Germans other things which apply in the first place only to us. In the spirit of which these addresses are the expression, I perceive that organic unity in which no member regards the fate of another as the fate of a stranger. I behold that unity (which shall and must arise if we are not to perish altogether) already achieved, completed, and existing.

*   *   *

. . . He who lets himself go without paying heed to himself, and allows himself to be moulded by circumstances just as they please, soon accustoms himself to any possible order of things. However much his eye may have been offended by something when he first saw it, let it only present itself anew every day in the same way and he accustoms himself to it. Later, he finds it natural, and in the end he even gets to like it as something inevitable; he would not thank you for the restoration of the original and better state of things, because this would tear him out of the mode of life to which he has become accustomed. In this way men become accustomed even to slavery, if only their material existence is not thereby affected, and in time they get to like it. It is just this that is the most dangerous thing about a state of subjection; it makes men insensitive to all true honour, and, moreover, for the indolent man it has its very pleasant side, because it relieves him of many a care and of the need of thinking for himself.

Let us be on our guard against being taken unawares by this sweetness of servitude, for it robs even our posterity of the hope of future emancipation. If our external activity is restricted and fettered, let us elevate our spirit all the more boldly to the thought of freedom; let us rise to live in this thought and make it the sole object of our wish and longing. What if freedom disappear for a time from the visible world? Let us give it a place of refuge in our innermost thoughts, until there shall grow up round about us the new world which has the power of manifesting our thoughts outwardly. In the sphere where no one can deprive us of the freedom to do as we think best—in our own minds let us make ourselves a pattern, a prophecy, and a guarantee of that which will become a reality when we are gone. Let us not allow our spirit, as well as our body, to be bent and subjected and brought into captivity.

If you ask me how this is to be brought about, the only entirely comprehensive answer is this: We must at once become what we ought to be in any case, namely, Germans. We are not to subject our spirit; therefore we must before all things provide a spirit for ourselves, and a firm and certain spirit; we must become earnest in all things and not go on existing frivolously, as if life were a jest; we must form for ourselves enduring and unshakable principles which will serve as a sure guide for all the rest of our thoughts and actions. Life and thought with us must be of one piece and a solid and interpenetrating whole; in both we must live according to nature and truth, and throw away foreign contrivances; in a word, we must provide character for ourselves; for to have character and to be German [*Charakter haben und deutsch sein*] undoubtedly mean the same; and the thing has no special name in our language, because it is intended to proceed immediately from our very existence without any knowledge or reflection on our part.

We must first of all set our own thoughts to work and think about the great events of our days, their relation to us, and what we have to expect from them; and we must provide ourselves with a firm and clear view of all these matters, and a definite and unchangeable Yes or No in answer to the questions that arise out of them. Everyone who makes the slightest claim to culture is bound to do that. The animal life of man proceeds in all ages according to the same laws, and in this every age is alike. Only to the understanding are there such things as different ages; and only the man whose conception penetrates them lives in them, and only he exists in his own age; any other kind of life is nothing but the life of plants and animals. To let everything that happens pass by one unperceived, perhaps to close eye and ear diligently to its urgent message, and even to boast of such thoughtlessness as if it were great wisdom—this may be the proper thing for a rock on which the waves of the sea beat without its feeling them, or for a tree-trunk dashed to and fro by storms without its perceiving them; but in no wise does it beseem a thinking being. Even the thinker who dwells in the higher spheres is not absolved from this general obligation of understanding his own age. Everything that is on the higher plane must want to influence the immediate present in its own fashion; and he who truly lives in the former lives at the same time in the latter also; if he did not live in the latter also, it would be a proof that he did not live in the former either, but only dreamed in it. That lack of heed to what is going on before our eyes, and the artful distraction to other objects of the attention that is everywhere aroused, would be the best thing that an enemy of our independence could wish to find. If he is sure that nothing will set us thinking, he can do anything he wishes with us, as if we were lifeless tools. It is precisely this thoughtlessness that accustoms itself to anything; but where clear and comprehensive thought, and in that thought the image of what ought to be, always remains watchful, there is no question of becoming accustomed to such things.

These addresses have in the first place invited you, and they will invite the whole German nation, in so far as it is possible at the present time to

assemble the nation around a speaker by means of the printed book, to come
to a definite decision and to be at one with themselves in their own minds on
the following questions:

1. Whether it is true or untrue that there is a German nation, and that its
   continued existence in its peculiar and independent nature is at the
   present time in danger;
2. Whether it is worth the trouble, or not worth the trouble, to maintain this
   nation;
3. Whether there is any sure and thorough means of maintaining it, and what
   this means is.

*   *   *

If only the German nation had remained united, with a common will
and a common strength! Then, though the other Europeans might have
wanted to murder each other on every sea and shore, and on every island too,
in the middle of Europe the firm wall of the Germans would have prevented
them from reaching each other. Here peace would have remained, and the
Germans would have maintained themselves, and with themselves also a
part of the other European peoples, in quiet and prosperity.

That things should remain thus did not suit the selfishness of foreign
countries, whose calculations did not look more than one moment ahead.
They found German bravery useful in waging their wars and German
hands useful to snatch the booty from their rivals. A means had to be found
to attain this end, and foreign cunning won an easy victory over German
ingenuousness and lack of suspicion. It was foreign countries which first
made use of the division of mind produced by religious disputes in Germany
—Germany, which presented on a small scale the features of Christian
Europe as a whole—foreign countries, I say, made use of these disputes to
break up the close inner unity of Germany into separate and disconnected
parts. Foreign countries had already destroyed their own unity naturally, by
splitting into parts over a common prey; and now they artificially destroyed
German unity. They knew how to present each of these separate States that
had thus arisen in the lap of the one nation—which had no enemy except
those foreign countries themselves, and no concern except the common one
of setting itself with united strength against their seductive craft and cunning—foreign countries, I say, knew how to present each of these States to
the others as a natural enemy, against which each State must be perpetually
on its guard. On the other hand, they knew how to make themselves appear
to the German States as natural allies against the danger threatening them
from their own countrymen—as allies with whom alone they would themselves stand or fall, and whose enterprises they must in turn support with all
their might. It was only because of this artificial bond that all the disputes
which might arise about any matter whatever in the Old World or the New

became disputes of the German races in their relation to each other. Every war, no matter what its cause, had to be fought out on German soil and with German blood; every disturbance of the balance had to be adjusted in that nation to which the whole fountainhead of such relationship was unknown; and the German States, whose separate existence was in itself contrary to all nature and reason, were compelled, in order that they might count for something, to act as make-weights to the chief forces in the scale of the European equilibrium, whose movement they followed blindly and without any will of their own. Just as in many States abroad the citizens are designated as belonging to this or that foreign party, or voting for this or that foreign alliance, but no name is found for those who belong to the party of their own country, so it was with the Germans; for long enough they belonged only to some foreign party or other, and one seldom came across a man who supported the party of the Germans and was of the opinion that this country ought to make an alliance with itself.

This, then, is the true origin and meaning, this the result for Germany and for the world, of that notorious doctrine of a balance of power to be artificially maintained between the European States. If Christian Europe had remained one, as it ought to be and as it originally was, there would never have been any occasion to think of such a thing. That which is one rests upon itself and supports itself, and does not split up into conflicting forces which must be brought to an equilibrium. Only when Europe became divided and without a law did the thought of a balance acquire a meaning from necessity. To this Europe, divided and without a law, Germany did not belong. If only Germany at any rate had remained one, it would have rested on itself in the centre of the civilized world like the sun in the centre of the universe; it would have kept itself at peace, and with itself the adjacent countries; and without any artificial measures it would have kept everything in equilibrium by the mere fact of its natural existence. It was only the deceit of foreign countries that dragged Germany into their own lawlessness and their own disputes; it was they who taught Germany the treacherous notion of the balance of power, for they knew it to be one of the most effective means of deluding Germany as to its own true advantage and of keeping it in that state of delusion. This aim is now sufficiently attained, and the result that was intended is now complete before our eyes. Even if we cannot do away with this result, why should we not at any rate extirpate the source of it in our own understanding, which is now almost the only thing over which we still have sovereign power? Why should the old dream still be placed before our eyes, now that disaster has awakened us from sleep? Why should we not now at any rate see the truth and perceive the only means that could have saved us? Perhaps our descendants may do what we see ought to be done, just as we now suffer because our fathers dreamed. Let us understand that the conception of an equilibrium to be artificially maintained might have been a consoling dream for foreign countries amid the guilt and evil that oppressed them; but that this conception, being an entirely foreign product, ought never to have taken root in the mind of a German, and that the Germans ought never to have been so situated that it could take root among them. Let us understand that now at any rate we must perceive the utter worthlessness of such a conception, and must see that the salvation of all is to be found, not in it, but solely in the unity of the Germans among themselves.

*   *   *

Now, at last, let us be bold enough to look at the deceptive vision of a universal monarchy, which people are beginning to hold up for public veneration in place of that equilibrium which for some time has been growing more and more preposterous, and let us perceive how hateful and contrary to reason that vision is. Spiritual nature was able to present the essence of humanity in extremely diverse gradations in individuals and in individuality as a whole, in peoples. Only when each people, left to itself, develops and forms itself in accordance with its own peculiar quality, and only when in every people each individual develops himself in accordance with that common quality, as well as in accordance with his own peculiar quality—then, and then only, does the manifestation of divinity appear in its true mirror as it ought to be; and only a man who either entirely lacks the notion of the rule of law and divine order, or else is an obdurate enemy thereto, could take upon himself to want to interfere with that law, which is the highest law in the spiritual world. Only in the invisible qualities of nations, which are hidden from their own eyes—qualities as the means whereby these nations remain in touch with the source of original life—only therein is to be found the guarantee of their present and future worth, virtue, and merit. If these qualities are dulled by admixture and worn away by friction, the flatness that results will bring about a separation from spiritual nature, and this in its turn will cause all men to be fused together to their uniform and conjoint destruction. As for the writers who console us for all our ills with the prospect that we, too, shall be subjects of the new universal monarchy that is beginning—are we to believe them when they say that someone or other has decided upon such a grinding together of all the germs of what is human in humanity, in order to press the unresisting dough into some new form, and that so monstrous an act of brutality or enmity against the human race is possible in this age of ours? Even if, in the first place, we were willing to make up our minds to believe such an utterly incredible thing, the further question arises: By what instrument is such a plan to be carried out? What sort of people is it to be which, in the present state of European culture, shall conquer the world for some new universal monarch?

*   *   *

The ideas we have mentioned, and all ideas of this kind, are products of a form of thinking which merely plays a game with itself and sometimes, too, gets caught in its own cobwebs—a form of thinking which is unworthy of German thoroughness and earnestness. At best, some of these ideas, as, for example, that of a political equilibrium, are serviceable guiding-lines to enable one to find one's way about in the extensive and confused multiplicity of phenomena and to set it in order; but to believe that these things exist in nature, or to strive to realize them, is the same as to expect to find the poles, the meridians, and the tropics, by which our survey of the earth is guided, actually marked and indicated on the surface of the globe. May it become the custom in our nation, not merely to think idly and as it were experimentally, just to see what will come of it, but to think in such a way that what we think shall be true and have a real effect in life! Then it will be superfluous to warn people against such phantoms of a political wisdom whose origin is foreign and which only deludes the Germans.

This thoroughness, earnestness, and weightiness in our way of thinking, once we have made it our own, will show itself in our life as well. We are defeated; whether we are now to be despised as well, and rightly despised, whether in addition to all other losses we are to lose our honour also—that will still depend on ourselves. The fight with weapons has ended; there arises now, if we so will it, the new fight of principles, of morals, of character.

Let us give our guests a picture of faithful devotion to friends and fatherland, of incorruptible uprightness and love of duty, of all civic and domestic virtues, to take home with them as a friendly gift from their hosts; for they will return home at last some time or other. Let us be careful not to invite them to despise us; there would, however, be no surer way for us to do this than if we either feared them beyond measure or gave up our own way of life and strove to resemble them in theirs. Be it far from us as individuals to be so unmannerly as to provoke or irritate individuals; but, as to the rest, our safest measure will be to go our own way in all things, as if we were alone with ourselves, and not to establish any relation that is not laid upon us by absolute necessity; and the surest means to this will be for each one to content himself with what the old national conditions are able to afford him, to take up his share of the common burden according to his powers, but to look upon any favour from foreigners as a disgrace and a dishonour.

In 1813, the Germans, led by the Prussians, rose up against their French conquerors and contributed significantly to the downfall of Napoleon. Some of the veterans of this war returned to their studies at the universities, inspired with the ideal they had served. They banded together into a fraternal organization, the Allgemeine Deutsche Burschen-

schaft, *which was intended to keep their ideal alive. It is
expressed in the two selections that follow.*

*This speech by theology student Riemann, Knight of
the Iron Cross, was delivered in the Hall of the Min-
nesingers at the Wartburg, October 18, 1817.*

Theology Student Riemann's Speech

MY ASSEMBLED BROTHERS, today for the fourth time the bonfire will
flame up to heaven, to remind us of the past and to urge us on to the future.
Since that battle, four long years have passed; the German people held fine
hopes then, but these have all been dissipated. The event has betrayed our
expectation; many a great and glorious task, which could have been accomplished and which must be accomplished, has been left undone; many a holy
and noble passion has been contaminated by contempt and scorn. Of all the
princes of Germany, only one has made good the pledge he gave—he, in
whose free land we celebrate the battle festival. Many a stouthearted man has
grown discouraged with such an outcome; many a man thinks that the
much-praised nobility of the German people has no meaning, withdraws
from the public life which showed such glorious promise, and seeks compen-
sation in the silent pursuit of science.

Others prefer to seek a new fatherland, in the far regions of the earth
where new life stirs.

But now I ask you who are gathered here, in the bloom of youth, with all
the enthusiasm supplied by the fresh young force of life—you who one day
will be the teachers, the representatives and the magistrates of the people,
upon whom the fatherland bases its hopes—you who have fought, some with
weapons in hand, but all in spirit and will, for the weal of the fatherland—I
ask you whether you are at one with such sentiments. No! Now and always,
no! In times of need we saw God's will and followed it. And that which we
recognized then we will hold to now, as long as a drop of blood runs in our
veins. The spirit which has brought us together here, the spirit of truth and
justice, shall lead us through all our life, that we, all brothers and sons of one
and the same fatherland, may build a brazen wall against the internal and
external enemies of that fatherland; that raging death may not affright us in
the open fight or make us fear to endure the fiercest onslaught when the
aggressor threatens; that when truth and justice are at stake, the glory of

P. Joachimsen, ed., *Die Nationalbewegung von 1815–49* (1928), translated in T. C. Mendenhall, B. D. Henning, and A. S. Foord, *The Quest for a Principle of Authority in Europe
1715–Present* (1948), pp. 208–9. Reprinted by permission of Holt, Rinehart and Winston, Inc.

thrones of kings may not blind us [to our duty] of speaking the strong free word—and that in our hearts the desire for truth, the desire for every human and patriotic virtue, may never be extinguished!

> *This charter was announced on the 18th day of the Month of Victory, 1818.*

Constitutional Charter of the Universal German Burschenschaft

I.

THE UNIVERSAL GERMAN *Burschenschaft* is the free association of all young German scholars, who are now being educated in the *Hochschule,* in one union, founded upon the relationship of German youth to the growing unity of the German people.

II.

As a free community, the Universal German *Burschenschaft* sets forth the following principles as the focus of its activity: (*a*) unity, freedom, and the mutual equality of all *Burschen;* equality of all rights and duties: (*b*) the development of all our spiritual and physical powers for the service of the fatherland, according to German-Christian principles.

III.

The companionship of all German *Burschen* in the spirit of these propositions represents the highest ideal of the Universal German *Burschenschaft:* the spiritual and physical union of all German *Burschen.*

IV.

The Universal German *Burschenschaft* comes into existence in this way, so that it may present, increasingly as time goes on, a model of a people prospering in freedom and unity, that it may maintain, in the development

P. Joachimsen, ed., *Die Nationalbewegung von 1815–49* (1928), translated in T. C. Mendenhall, B. D. Henning, and A. S. Foord, *The Quest for a Principle of Authority in Europe 1715–Present* (1948), pp. 208–9. Reprinted by permission of Holt, Rinehart and Winston, Inc.

of all spiritual and physical forces, a national brotherly way of life, and may prepare its members for public life in this free, equal, and orderly community, with the end that each of them will be exalted to such a grade of self-assurance that his pure individuality will reflect the noble glory of German folk life.

3 The Confrontation of Liberalism and Nationalism

Carl Schurz, born in 1829, represented a generation once removed from the stirring events of 1813. In 1848 he was a student, a liberal, and a nationalist. The three seemed perfectly compatible then; Schurz was soon to find that, as conditions changed, certain strains were introduced. Ultimately, Schurz fled Germany and came to the United States.

In the selection that follows, Schurz gives his analysis of German history to 1848 and an account of what happened then.

FROM *The Reminiscences of Carl Schurz*

THEN CAME, IN 1813, after long suffering and debasement, the great popular uprising against Napoleonic despotism, and with it a period of a new German national consciousness. To this feeling appealed the famous manifesto, issued from the town of Kalisch, in which the king of Prussia, allied with the Russian Czar, after Napoleon's defeat in Russia, called the German people to arms, promising at the same time a new national union and participation of the people in the business of government under constitutional forms. The new birth of a united German national empire, the abolition of arbitrary government by the introduction of free political institutions—that was the solemn promise of the Prussian king as the people understood it—that was the hope which inspired the people in the struggle against Napoleonic rule with enthusiastic heroism and a self-sacrifice without limit, and ended in a final victory. It was one of the periods in history when a people proved itself ready to sacrifice all for the attainment of an ideal. But after the victories of Leipzig and Waterloo followed another time

The Reminiscences of Carl Schurz, I (1907), 103–6, 109–10, 112–4, 118–21, 124–6, 134–8, 141–5, 154–6, 161–3.

of bitter disappointment. Against the formation of a united Germany arose not only the jealous opposition of non-German Europe, but also the selfish ambitions of the smaller German princes, especially of those who, as members of the "Rheinbund," such as Bavaria, Würtemberg, Baden, etc., had been raised in their rank. And this opposition was strengthened by the intriguing policy of Austria, which, with her possessions outside of Germany, had also un-German interests and designs. And this Austrian policy was conducted by Prince Metternich, the prime minister of Austria, to whom every emotion of German patriotism was foreign, as he hated and feared every free aspiration among the people. Thus the peace was far from bringing to the German people the reward for their sacrifices which they had deserved and expected. From the Congress of Vienna, in 1814 and 1815, which disposed of peoples as of herds of cattle in order to establish a permanent balance of power in Europe, nothing issued for the German nation but a treaty of alliance between German states, the famous "Deutsche Bund," the organ of which was to be the "Bundestag"; and this organ was to be composed of the representatives of the various German kings and princes, without any vestige of a representation of the people. There was no mention of any guarantee of civic rights, of a popular vote, of a free press, of the freedom of assembly, of a trial by jury. On the contrary, the "Bundestag," impotent as an organ of the German nation in its relations to the outside world, developed itself only as a mutual insurance society of despotic rulers— as a central police board for the suppression of all national and liberal movements. The king of Prussia, Frederick William III, the same who had made the promises to the people contained in the proclamation of Kalisch, had probably in the days of distress and of national uprising honestly meant to do what he promised. But his mind was narrow and easily disposed to consider autocratic authority on his part as necessary for the well-being of the world. . . .

Hope revived when Frederick William III's son and successor, Frederick William IV, ascended the Prussian throne in 1840. He was regarded as a man of high intelligence and had, as crown-prince, excited fair expectations. Many considered him incapable of continuing the stupid and sterile policy of his father. Indeed, the first utterances of the new king and the employment of able men in high positions encouraged the hope that he harbored a national heart, in sympathy with the patriotic aspirations of the German people, and that the liberal currents of the time would find in him appreciative understanding. But fresh disappointment followed. As soon as the demand was publicly made, that now at last the old promises of a representative government should be fulfilled, the king's attitude changed. These demands were bluntly repelled, and the censorship of the press was enforced with renewed severity.

*   *   *

There had indeed long been some revolutionary agitators who, in their isolation, had passed for dreamers and could win but a slim following. But now the feeling began to spread in large circles that the real thunder-storm was coming, although hardly anybody anticipated how soon it would come. In former days people had excited themselves about what Thiers and Guizot had said in the French chambers, or Palmerston and Derby in the English parliament, or even what Hecker, Rotteck and Welker had said in the little Diet of the grand duchy of Baden. But now everybody listened with nervous eagerness to every word that in the United Diet of the most important of German states had fallen from the lips of Camphausen, Vincke, Beckerath, Hansemann and other liberal leaders. There was a feeling in the air as if this United Diet, in its position and the task to be performed by it, was not at all unlike the French assembly of the year 1789.

We university students watched these events with perhaps a less clear understanding, but with no less ardent interest, than our elders. As I have already mentioned, the "Burschenschaft" had its political traditions. Immediately after the wars of liberation—1813 to 1815—it had been among the first in line to raise the cry for the fulfillment of the pledges given by the princes. It had cultivated the national spirit with zeal, although sometimes with exaggerated demonstrations. It had furnished many victims in the persecutions of so-called demagogues. The political activity of the old Burschenschaft had indeed not been continued by the younger associations; but "God, Liberty, Fatherland," had still remained the common watchword; we still wore the prohibited black-red-golden ribbon under our coats, and very many members of the new Burschenschaft societies still recognized it as their duty to keep themselves well informed of what happened in the political world and to devote to it as active an interest as possible. Thus the liberal currents of our time found among us enthusiastic partisans, although we young people could not give a very definite account of the practical steps to be taken.

In the prosecution of my studies I had taken up with ardor the history of Europe at the period of the great Reformation. I expected to make this my specialty as a professor of history. The great characters of that period strongly attracted me and I could not resist the temptation to clothe some of them in dramatic form. So I planned a tragedy, the main figure of which was to be Ulrich von Hutten, and I began to elaborate some scenes in detail.

*   *   *

One morning, toward the end of February, 1848, I sat quietly in my attic-chamber, working hard at my tragedy of "Ulrich von Hutten," when suddenly a friend rushed breathlessly into the room, exclaiming: "What, you sitting here! Do you not know what has happened?"

"No; what?"

"The French have driven away Louis Philippe and proclaimed the republic."

I threw down my pen—and that was the end of "Ulrich von Hutten." I never touched the manuscript again. We tore down the stairs, into the street, to the market-square, the accustomed meeting-place for all the student societies after their midday dinner. Although it was still forenoon, the market was already crowded with young men talking excitedly. There was no shouting, no noise, only agitated conversation. What did we want there? This probably no one knew. But since the French had driven away Louis Philippe and proclaimed the republic, something of course must happen here, too. Some of the students had brought their rapiers along, as if it were necessary at once to make an attack or to defend ourselves. We were dominated by a vague feeling as if a great outbreak of elemental forces had begun, as if an earthquake was impending of which we had felt the first shock, and we instinctively crowded together. Thus we wandered about in numerous bands—to the "Kneipe," where our restlessness, however, would not suffer us long to stay; then to other pleasure resorts, where we fell into conversation with all manner of strangers, to find in them the same confused, astonished and expectant state of mind; then back to the market-square, to see what might be going on there; then again somewhere else, and so on, without aim and end, until finally late in the night fatigue compelled us to find the way home.

The next morning there were the usual lectures to be attended. But how profitless! The voice of the professor sounded like a monotonous drone coming from far away. What he had to say did not seem to concern us. The pen that should have taken notes remained idle. At last we closed with a sigh the notebook and went away, impelled by a feeling that now we had something more important to do—to devote ourselves to the affairs of the fatherland. And this we did by seeking as quickly as possible again the company of our friends, in order to discuss what had happened and what was to come. In these conversations, excited as they were, certain ideas and catchwords worked themselves to the surface, which expressed more or less the feelings of the people. Now had arrived in Germany the day for the establishment of "German Unity," and the founding of a great, powerful national German Empire. In the first line the convocation of a national parliament. Then the demands for civil rights and liberties, free speech, free press, the right of free assembly, equality before the law, a freely elected representation of the people with legislative power, responsibility of ministers, self-government of the communes, the right of the people to carry arms, the formation of a civic guard with elective officers, and so on—in short, that which was called a "constitutional form of government on a broad democratic basis." Republican ideas were at first only sparingly expressed. But the word democracy was soon on all tongues, and many, too, thought it a matter of course that if the princes should try to withhold from the people the rights and liberties demanded, force would take the place of mere petition. Of course the regeneration of the fatherland must, if possible, be accomplished by peaceable means. A few days after the outbreak of this commotion I reached my nineteenth birthday. I remember to have been so entirely absorbed by what was happening that I could hardly turn my thoughts to anything else. Like many of my friends, I was dominated by the feeling that at last the great opportunity had arrived for giving to the German people the liberty which was their birthright and to the German fatherland its unity and greatness, and that it was now the first duty of every German to do and to sacrifice everything for this sacred object. We were profoundly, solemnly in earnest.

* * *

The enthusiastic elation was followed by a short time of anxious expectancy. At last came the report of the awful events that had taken place in the capital.

The king of Prussia, Frederick William IV, at first received the petitions rushing in upon him with sullen silence. He had so recently, and then so emphatically, even so defiantly, proclaimed his inflexible determination never to consent to any constitutional limitation of his kingly power, that the thought of yielding to popular pressure anything that he fancied should be only a free emanation of the royal will was well-nigh inconceivable to him. But the situation became more threatening from day to day. Not only the language of the deputations arriving from various parts of the kingdom constantly grew more and more impetuous and peremptory, but the people of Berlin began to hold mass meetings counting by thousands and to greet with thundering acclamations the political watchwords uttered by popular orators. The municipal authorities, too, were swept into the current and entreated the king to make concessions. At last he saw the necessity of yielding something. On the 14th of March he gave a "gracious" answer to an address presented by the city council, but that answer was still too evasive and indefinite to satisfy public opinion. Meanwhile bloody collisions occurred between the police supported by military detachments and the multitude thronging the public squares and streets, in which a merchant and a university student were killed. The bitterness of feeling caused by these events was somewhat assuaged by a rumor that the king had resolved upon further and more important concessions, which would be publicly announced on the 18th. He had indeed concluded to issue an edict opening a prospect of steps to be taken in favor of national unity and abolishing the censorship of the press.

On the afternoon of the fateful 18th of March an immense concourse of people assembled on the open square in front of the royal palace, hoping to hear the authoritative announcement that the popular demands had been granted. The king appeared on the balcony and was received with enthusiastic cheers. He attempted to speak, but could not be heard. In the belief, however, that he had granted all that was asked for, the people were ready for a jubilee. Then a cry arose for the removal of the bodies of troops surrounding the palace and appearing to separate the king from his people. It seemed to be expected that this would be granted, too, for an effort was made to open a passage for the soldiers through the dense crowd, when a roll of drums was heard. This was regarded as a signal for the departure of the soldiery; but, instead of the troops withdrawing, heavy bodies of infantry and cavalry pressed upon the multitude for the evident purpose of clearing the square. Then two shots rang from the infantry line and the whole scene suddenly and frightfully changed. Frantic cries arose: "We are betrayed! We are betrayed!" In an instant the mass of people who but a moment before had joyously acclaimed the king, dispersed in the adjoining streets with the angry shout, "To arms, to arms!" In all directions the thoroughfares were soon blocked with barricades. The pavingstones seemed to leap from the ground and to form themselves into bulwarks surmounted by black-red-gold flags, and manned by citizens, university students, tradesmen, artists, laborers, professional men—hastily armed with all sorts of weapons, from rifles and shotguns down to pikes, axes and hammers. There was no preparation, no plan, no system, in the uprising; everybody seemed to follow a common instinct. Then the troops were ordered to the assault. When, after a fierce fight they had taken one barricade, they were at short distances confronted by another and another. Behind the barricades women were busy bringing food and drink for the fighters and caring for the wounded. During the whole night the city resounded with the roar of cannon and the rattle of musketry.

The king seemed at first sternly determined to put down the insurrection at any cost; but as the street battle proceeded he became painfully conscious of its terrible character. Reports arrived in rapid succession. He would now give an order to stop the fight and then an order to go on. Shortly after midnight he wrote with his own hand an address to "My dear Berliners." He began by saying that the firing of the two shots which had caused the excitement had been a mere accident, that a band of miscreants, mostly foreigners, had taken advantage of this misunderstanding to goad many of his good subjects into the fratricidal fight. Then he promised to withdraw the troops as soon as the insurgents would remove the barricades, and he implored them "to listen to the fatherly voice of their king, to which the grievously suffering queen joined her affectionate and tearful prayers." But the address failed to produce the desired effect. It was accompanied with the roar of cannon and the rattle of musketry, and the fighting citizens rather resented being called "a band of miscreants."

At last, on the afternoon of Sunday, the 19th of March, when one of the high commanders of the troops, General Möllendorf, had been captured by the citizens, the withdrawal of the troops was resolved upon. Peace was concluded on the understanding that the army should leave Berlin, that there should be freedom of the press, and that Prussia should have a constitution on a broad democratic basis. When the soldiery had marched off something happened that in dramatic force and significance has never been surpassed in the history of revolutions. From all parts of the city solemn and silent processions moved toward the royal palace. They escorted the bodies of those of the people who had been killed in the battle; the corpses of the slain were carried aloft on litters, their gaping wounds uncovered, their heads wreathed with laurel branches and immortelles. So the processions marched into the inner palace court, where the litters were placed in rows in ghastly parade, and around them the multitude of men with pallid faces, begrimed with blood and powder smoke, many of them still carrying the weapons with which they had fought during the night; and among them women and children bewailing their dead. Then the king was loudly called for. He appeared in an open gallery, pale and dejected, by his side the weeping queen. "Hat off!" the multitude shouted, and the king took off his hat to the dead below. Then a deep voice among the crowd intoned the old hymn, "Jesus, meine Zuversicht"—"Jesus, my Refuge," in which all present joined. The chorus finished, the king silently withdrew and the procession moved away in grim solemnity.

*   *   *

Suddenly after a prolonged fermentation, and following an impulse from abroad, the German people rose up in strength. The kings and princes now conceded everything that they had refused before, and the people found themselves all at once in full possession of an unaccustomed power. Is it to be wondered at that these surprising changes brought forth some confused desires and misdirected endeavors? Would it not have been more astonishing if the people had at once clearly defined and wisely limited their desires, and promptly found the right means for the attainment of the right objects? Do we expect that the beggar who suddenly becomes a millionaire will instantly know how to make the best use of his unwonted wealth? And yet, it cannot be said of the large majority of the German people that, however vague their political notions may have been, they asked in the revolutionary movements of the year 1848 in the main for anything that was unreasonable or unattainable. Much of what they at that period sought to accomplish has since been realized. The errors committed by them in 1848 were more in the means employed than in the ends aimed at. And the greatest of these errors sprang from the childlike confidence with which they expected the complete fulfillment of all the promises which the kings and princes, especially the King of Prussia, had made under stress of circumstances. It is idle to indulge in speculations about that which might have been if that which was had been different. But one thing is certain: If the princes had not permitted themselves to be seduced by the machinations of the reactionary parties on the one side, nor to be frightened by occasional popular excesses on the other, but had with unflinching fidelity and with the exertion of all their power done that which in March, 1848, they had given the people reason to expect of them, the essential objects fought for at that period would have proved themselves entirely practicable. It was indeed not prudent on the part of the people in their enthusiastic enjoyment of what they called the "Volkerfrühling"—the People's Springtime—an enjoyment to which they gave themselves with such ingenuous elation, to cherish that credulous confidence, instead of assuring themselves of the necessary guarantees against a reaction bound to come; but this imprudence sprang from no ignoble source. He surely wrongs the German people who lays solely at their and their leaders' doors the responsibility for the failures of the years 1848–49, overlooking the tergiversations of the princes.

*   *   *

The national parliament at Frankfurt elected in the spring, which represented the sovereignty of the German people in the large sense and was to give to the united German nation a national government, counted among its members a great many men illustrious in the fields, not of politics, but of science and literature. It soon showed a dangerous tendency of squandering in brilliant, but more or less fruitless, debates much of the time which was sorely needed for prompt and decisive action to secure the legitimate results of the revolution against hostile forces.

But our eyes were turned still more anxiously upon Berlin. Prussia was by far the strongest of the purely German states. The Austrian empire was a conglomeration of different nationalities—German, Magyar, Slavic and Italian. The German element, to which the dynasty and the political capital belonged, had so far been the predominant one. It was most advanced in civilization and wealth, although inferior in numbers. But the Slavs, the Magyars and the Italians, stimulated by the revolutionary movements of 1848, were striving for national autonomy, and although Austria had held the foremost place in the later periods of the ancient German empire and then after the Napoleonic wars in the German Confederacy, it seemed problematic whether her large non-German interests would permit her to play a leading part now in the political unification of Germany under a constitutional government. In fact, it turned out subsequently that the mutual jealousies of the different races enabled the Austrian central government to subjugate to despotic rule one by the other, in spite of the hopeful beginnings of the revolution, and that the non-German interests of Austria and those of the dynasty were predominant in her policy. But Prussia, excepting a comparatively small Polish district, was a purely German country, and by far the strongest among the German states in point of numbers, of general education, of economic activity and especially of military power. It was, therefore, generally felt that the attitude of Prussia would be decisive in determining the fate of the revolution.

For a while the Prussian king, Frederick William IV, seemed to be pleased with the rôle of a leader in the national movement which the revolution had made him assume. His volatile nature seemed to be warmed by a new enthusiasm. He took walks on the streets and talked freely with the people. He spoke of constitutional principles of government to be introduced as a matter of course. He loudly praised the noble generosity which the people of Berlin had manifested toward him in the hours of stress. He ordered the army to wear the black-red-gold cockade together with the Prussian. On the parade ground at Potsdam he declared to the sulking officers of the guards "that he felt himself perfectly safe, free and happy among the citizens of Berlin; that all the concessions made by him had been made of his own free will and according to his own convictions, and that nobody should dare to question this." But when the Prussian constituent assembly had met in Berlin and began to pass laws, and to design constitutional provisions, and to interfere with the conduct of the government in the spirit of the revolution, the king's mind gradually opened itself to other influences, and those influences gained access to him and surrounded him all the more readily since he removed his residence from Berlin to his palace at Potsdam, a little town preponderantly inhabited by courtiers and soldiers and other dependents of the government. Thus the king's immediate contact with the people ceased, his conferences with the newly appointed liberal ministers were confined to short formal "audiences," and voices appealing to old sympathies, prepossessions and partialities were constantly nearest to his ear.

There was the army, traditionally the pet of the Hohenzollerns, smarting under the "disgrace" of its withdrawal from Berlin after the street battle, and pining for revenge and restoration of its prestige. There was the court nobility, whose business it always had been to exalt and flatter the royal person. There was the landed aristocracy, the "Junker" element, whose feudal privileges were theoretically denied by the revolutionary spirit and practically invaded by the legislative action of the representatives of the people, and who artfully goaded the king's pride. There was the old bureaucracy, the power of which had been broken by the revolution, although its personnel had but little been changed, and which sought to recover its former sway. There was the "old Prussian" spirit which resented any national aspirations that might encroach upon the importance and self-appreciation of specific Prussiandom, and which still had strength in the country immediately surrounding Berlin and in some of the eastern provinces. All these forces, which in a general term were popularly called "the reaction," worked together to divert the king from the course he had ostensibly taken immediately after the revolution of March, with the hope of using him for the largest possible restoration of the old order of things—well knowing that if they controlled him, they would, through him, control the army, and then with it a tremendous, perhaps decisive, force in the conflicts to come. And this "reaction" was greatly strengthened by the cunning exploitation of some street excesses that happened in Berlin—excesses which in a free country like England might, indeed, have brought forth some vigorous measures of repression by the police, but would certainly not have induced anybody to call the practicability of civil freedom or of the constitutional principles of government in question. But these occurrences were used in Prussia with considerable effect to frighten the timid men of the bourgeoisie with the specter of general anarchy, and to persuade the king that after all the restoration of unrestrained royal power was necessary for the maintenance of law and order.

On the other hand, the visible development of the reaction had the effect of producing among many of those who stood earnestly for national unity and constitutional government, a state of mind more open to radical tendencies. The rapid progress of these developments was clearly perceptible in my own surroundings. Our democratic club was composed in almost equal parts of students and citizens, among whom there were many of excellent character, of some fortune and good standing, and of moderate views, while a few others had worked themselves into a state of mind resembling that of the terrorists in the French Revolution. Kinkel was the recognized leader of the club, and I soon became a member of the executive committee. At first the establishment of a constitutional monarchy with universal suffrage and well-secured civil rights would have been quite satisfactory to us. But the reaction, the threatened rise of which we were observing, gradually made many of us believe that there was no safety for popular liberty except in a republic. From this belief there was only one step to the further conclusion, that in a republic, and only in a republic, all evils of the social body could be cured, and the solution of all the political problems would be possible. The idealism which saw in the republican citizen the highest embodiment of human dignity we had imbibed from the study of classic antiquity; and the history of the French Revolution satisfied us that a republic could be created in Germany and could maintain its existence in the European system of states. In that history we found striking examples of the possibility of accomplishing the seemingly impossible, if only the whole energy resting in a great nation were awakened and directed with unflinching boldness. Most of us indeed recoiled from the wild excesses which had stained with streams of innocent blood the national uprising in France during the Reign of Terror. But we hoped to stir up the national energies without such terrorism. At any rate the history of the French Revolution furnished to us models in plenty that mightily excited our imagination. How dangerously seductive such a play of the imagination is, we were of course then unaware.

*   *   *

On a bright September morning I sailed up the Rhine from Bonn to Mainz. I should have enjoyed it with the fullness of youthful spirits had I been able to drive away the disquieting thoughts which were stirred up by confused rumors of a riot and street-battle in Frankfurt. In fact, upon my arrival in that city I found those rumors distressingly verified.

The revolt in Frankfurt was the outcome of the following events. I have already mentioned that the popular uprising in the duchies of Holstein and Schleswig against the Danish rule had been sanctioned as a national cause by the old Diet of the German Confederation, and then by the national parliament and by all the several German governments. Prussian and other German troops had marched into the duchies and won considerable advantages over the Danish army on the field of battle. Everything promised a speedy and happy termination of the war. It was therefore a painful surprise when the Prussian government, whose head, Frederick William IV, had as usual permitted himself to be intimidated by the other European powers, concluded in the name of the German Confederation a truce with Denmark —the so-called "truce of Malmö"—in which it was agreed that the victorious German troops were to retire from the duchies, that the duchies were to lose their own provisional government, and that a commission composed of two Prussians, two Danes and a fifth member to be elected by them was to govern the disputed country. At the same time all the laws and ordinances that had been issued by the Schleswig-Holstein authorities since the days of March, 1848, were declared invalid. This truce called forth the greatest indignation all over Germany. The representative assembly of Schleswig-Holstein protested. The national parliament in Frankfurt, which saw not only the honor of Germany grievous compromised, but its own authority overruled by these proceedings of the Prussian government, resolved on September 5 to refuse the recognition of the truce of Malmö and to demand the suspension of all the measures stipulated therein. But after several failures to form a new ministry on the basis of this resolution, and not daring to bring the question of authority between itself and the Prussian government to a direct issue, the parliament revoked the resolution of September 5, ten days later, and declared at the same time that the execution of the truce of Malmö could apparently no longer be hindered. This declaration, which seemed to strike the sympathies of the German people full in the face, caused immense excitement, of which the revolutionary leaders in Frankfurt and the surrounding country at once took advantage. On the next day a large mass meeting was held on a meadow near Frankfurt. Inflammatory speeches goaded the passions of the multitude to fury, and the meeting adopted resolutions by which the members of the majority of the national parliament in Frankfurt were branded as traitors to the German nation. Troops of armed democrats poured in from all sides, and an attempt was made to force the parliament to revoke the hateful declaration, or to drive out the traitorous majority. Two prominent conservative members of the parliament, Count Auerswald and Prince Lichnowsky, fell into the hands of the revolutionists and were killed; and then followed a bloody struggle in the streets of Frankfurt, in which the insurgents soon succumbed to the quickly concentrated troops.

When on my way to Eisenach I arrived in Frankfurt, the victorious soldiery still bivouacked on the streets around their burning campfires; the barricades had not yet been removed; the pavement was still stained with blood, and everywhere the heavy tramp of military patrols was heard. With difficulty I made my way to the hotel "Zum Schwan," where I was to meet, according to agreement, some Heidelberg students, in order to continue in their company the journey to Eisenach. With hearts full of gloom we sat together deep into the night, for we all felt that the cause of liberty and of popular sovereignty had received a terrible blow. The royal Prussian government had successfully defied the national parliament, which represented the sovereignty of the German nation. Those who called themselves "the people" had made a hostile attempt upon the embodiment of popular sovereignty which had issued from the revolution, and this embodiment of popular sovereignty had been obliged to call upon the armed forces of the princes for protection against the hatred of "the people." Thus the backbone of the revolution begun in March, 1848, was substantially broken. We young students indeed did not see so far. But we felt that terrible mischief had been done. Our youthful spirits, however, consoled themselves with the hope that what was lost might still be recovered by well-directed and energetic action under more favorable circumstances.

The next day I visited with some of my friends the gallery of St. Paul's Church, in which the national parliament held its sessions. With that profound reverence, the organ of which (to express myself in the language of phrenology) has always been with me very strongly developed, I looked at that historic spot, in which the fate of the revolution of 1848 was already foretold. On "the right" there sat, with a smile of triumph on their lips, men whose principal aim it was to restore the old order of things; in "the center" the advocates of a liberal constitutional monarchy, tormented by anxious doubt as to whether they could control the revolutionary tendencies without making the absolutist reaction all-powerful; on "the left" the democrats and republicans with the oppressive consciousness that the masses of the people, in whom they were to find the source of their power, had grievously compromised them by this wild eruption of passion at Frankfurt and had thus put the most dangerous weapon into the hands of the reactionists.

I remember well the men whom my eyes most eagerly sought. On "the right" Radowitz, whose finely chiseled face, somewhat oriental in its character, looked like a sealed book containing the secret of reactionary politics; in "the center" Heinrich von Gagern, with his imposing stature and heavy eyebrows; on "the left" the Silenus-head of Robert Blum, whom many regarded as the ideal man of the people; and the little shriveled figure of the old poet, Ludwig Uhland, whose songs we had so often sung, and who with such touching fidelity stood by that which he believed to be the good right of his people!

*   *   *

Since March the Prussian government had moved in constitutional forms, and the ministry, at the head of which stood the liberal General von

Pfuel, showed itself willing to fulfill the promises that had been given. But the king and his immediate surroundings had on various occasions manifested a disposition which hardly harmonized with those pledges and called forth grave apprehensions. On October 31 the Prussian Constituent Assembly gave voice to the general sympathy with the struggling people of Vienna and resolved to request his Majesty's government "to take speedy and energetic steps to induce the German central power in Frankfurt to effectually protect the imperiled liberties of the people in the German districts of Austria, and to restore peace." The president of the ministry, General von Pfuel, supported this resolution. The next day he found himself compelled to resign, and the king then appointed a ministry of decidedly reactionary character, at the head of which he put Count Brandenburg, and the leading spirit of which was Herr von Manteuffel. The Constituent Assembly solemnly protested, but in vain. On November 9 the Brandenburg ministry presented itself to the Assembly with a royal message which transferred the meetings of that body to another place and prorogued its sessions until November 27. By a large majority the Assembly denied the right of the royal government to do these things, but the next day the house was surrounded by large bodies of troops under General Wrangel, who gave the order that nobody should be permitted to enter, but anybody might leave the building. On November 11 the civil guard of Berlin was dissolved and in a few days disarmed. The Assembly moved from one place to another, constantly followed by the soldiery, until finally on November 15, at its last meeting, it refused to vote the supplies, and declared "that this ministry had no right to dispose of the moneys of the state or to levy taxes, so long as the Constituent Assembly could not undisturbed continue its deliberations in Berlin." These events called forth immense excitement all over the country. They seemed to prove that the reactionary court-parties were determined to sweep away by force all the fruits of the revolution.

That the Constituent Assembly in opposing the "coup d'état" was altogether within its right, admitted of no doubt in the minds of the democrats. They blamed it only for not having made the fullest use of its right by calling the people directly to arms, and for having at this moment of great decision limited itself to the weak-kneed policy of "passive resistance." But they thought that this passive resistance by means of a general refusal to pay taxes might finally force the government to yield, assuming that the refusal to pay taxes would become general and be maintained with inflexible steadiness.

* * *

Now it appeared to us unnecessary to seize upon the general machinery of the tax-department. The next day a committee, of which I was a member, appeared at the city hall to take possession of it. The Burgomaster received us with great politeness and listened quietly to what we had to say to him about the authority of the Constituent Assembly and its power to stop the payment of taxes; but he tried to amuse us with all sorts of evasive talk. At last we became impatient and demanded an immediate and definite answer according to which we would resolve upon further measures. Suddenly we noticed a change in the expression of the Burgomaster's face. He seemed to hearken to something going on outside and then, still politely but with a sort of triumphant smile on his lips, he said: "Gentlemen, your answer you will have to receive from somebody else. Do you hear that?" Now we hearkened too, and heard a still distant, but approaching, sound of a military band playing the Prussian national air. The music sounded nearer and nearer in the street leading up from the Rhine. In a few minutes it reached the market-place and behind it came the heavy tramp of an infantry column which presently filled a large part of the square in front of the city hall. Our conversation with the Burgomaster of course came to a sudden end and we thought it very decent on his part that he permitted us to leave the building undisturbed.

*   *   *

Of the large parliamentary bodies that had issued from the revolution of March, only the national parliament in Frankfurt was still in existence. That existence it had owed to the longing of the German people, or rather the German peoples, for national unity, and it was its natural and universally understood mission to weld the German peoples under a common constitution of national government into one great nation. Immediately after the revolution of March, 1848, the different German governments, and with them also Austria, because of her German possessions, had recognized this object as a legitimate one, and it was with their co-operation that in May the elections for the national parliament had taken place. The large majority of that body, in fact, the German people in general, regarded the Frankfurt parliament as the specific representative of the sovereignty of the German nation. It was to be expected that the princes and those of their adherents, who may be designated as court-parties, would submit to this conception of the powers of the parliament only so long, and only so far, as they found themselves forced to do so. But few of the princes, if any, were sufficiently liberal to accept a limitation of their princely prerogatives with equanimity. Every gain of the people in the matter of political power they felt to be their own loss. Of course they were also opposed to the institution of a strong national government for the reason that this would be conditioned upon the surrender to the national authority of many of the sovereignty-rights of the different states. It was not only a national republic that the individual German sovereigns feared, but they also dreaded a national Kaiser who would be apt to reduce them to the condition of mere vassals. The German princes, with the exception of the one who could hope himself to occupy the imperial throne, were therefore the natural adversaries of German unity, embodied in a strong national government. There may have been some men of national sentiment among them capable of overcoming this reluctance, but certainly there were very few. Austria desired a united Germany in some form, only if it could hope to occupy in it the position of the leading power.

Face to face with the princes and their parties stood the national parliament in Frankfurt, that child of the revolution, which might then have almost been called the orphan of the revolution. It had at its immediate disposal no administrative machinery, no army, no treasury, only its moral authority; all the other things were in the hands of the different German state governments. The only power of the national parliament consisted in the will of the people. And this power was sufficient for the fulfillment of its mission so long as the will of the people proved itself strong enough, even through revolutionary action in case of necessity, to counteract the adverse interests of the princes. The parliament would have been sure of success in creating a constitutional German empire, if it had performed that task quickly and elected and put into office its Kaiser while the revolutionary prestige of the people was still unbroken—that is to say, in the first two or three months after the revolution of March. No German prince would then have declined the imperial crown with a constitution ever so democratic, and not one of them would have dared to refuse the sacrifice of any of his sovereignty-rights to the national power.

But that parliament was laboring under an overabundance of learning and virtue and under a want of that political experience and sagacity which recognizes that the better is often the enemy of the good, and that the true statesman will be careful not to imperil that which is essential by excessive insistence upon things which are of comparatively little consequence. The world has probably never seen a political assembly that contained a larger number of noble, learned, conscientious and patriotic men, and it will be difficult to find a book of the same character richer in profound knowledge and in models of lofty eloquence than its stenographic reports. But it did not possess the genius that promptly discerns opportunity and with quick resolution takes fortune by the forelock; it was not mindful of the fact that in times of great commotion the history of the world does not wait for the theoretical thinker. And thus it failed.

The failure of the Frankfurt Assembly was greeted with joy by the German conservatives who saw liberalism as the enemy. German unity, on the other hand, was something else again, and Otto von Bismarck, who was ultimately to lead Prussia to the dominant position in a united Germany, put the matter quite bluntly in his famous speech of 1862. It should be noted that rarely has a leader of a powerful nation expended less blood and utilized less iron in the successful pursuit of his policies than the "Iron Chancellor."

FROM *Otto von Bismarck's Speech to the Budget Commission*

OUR BLOOD IS TOO HOT; we prefer to wear armor which is too heavy for our slender body; but we should use it nonetheless. The eyes of Germany are fixed not upon Prussia's liberalism, but upon her armed might. Bavaria, Württemberg, and Baden may indulge in liberal experiments; therefore no one will assign to them Prussia's role. Prussia must harbor and maintain her strength for the favorable moment—a moment which has already, on one occasion, slipped by; Prussia's boundaries, as drawn by the Vienna treaties, are not suitable for a healthy state life. The great questions of the day will not be decided by speeches or by majority decisions—that was the mistake of 1848 and 1849—but by blood and iron!

In 1866, the Prussians, under the shrewd leadership of Otto von Bismarck, were able to provoke Austria into a war. In a few weeks it was all over, and Prussia emerged as undoubted leader of North Germany. The first striking victory on the road to German unity had been won.

Baumgarten was a German liberal who felt it necessary to re-examine the tenets of German liberalism in the light of the national triumph just achieved.

FROM *German Liberalism* BY H. BAUMGARTEN

IT WOULD BE OF CONSIDERABLE VALUE for us to be acquainted in detail with the historical development of liberalism in the years from 1815

P. Joachimsen, ed., *Die Nationalbewegung von 1815–49* (1928), translated in T. C. Mendenhall, B. D. Henning, and A. S. Foord, *The Quest for a Principle of Authority in Europe 1715–Present* (1948), p. 220. Reprinted by permission of Holt, Rinehart and Winston, Inc.

H. Baumgarten, "Der Deutsche Liberalismus, Eine Selbstkritik," *Preussische Jahrbücher*, 18 (1866), 468–79, 499–501, 507–12, translated by Eleanore L. Miller.

to 1848. . . . If we want to be honest, we must admit that during the period mentioned liberalism did indeed achieve much in the petty states. In individual states it considerably improved conditions in many respects and often prevented a turn for the worse. Above all, it kept alive the spirit of the nation and gave it its first political schooling. However, on the whole the liberal movement remained small, uninstructive, and unproductive. It could not grant the nation what it so desperately needed. Liberalism was not to blame for this; rather it was the circumstances. *In order to be effective within the state, the man must above all have a state; all those individual German territories, however, to which liberalism found itself confined because of the resignation of Prussia, were not states. . . .*

Justice demands the recognition of the fact that these petty states on the average accomplished more under the given circumstances than one in all probability could have predicted. Actually, only the modesty and conscientiousness of the Germans made it possible for this pitiful particularism on the whole to be efficient in administration. We owe it to the administration that a large part of the German people, in spite of the most unfavorable nature of the political situation, made gratifying progress economically and spiritually after 1815. The unselfishness and peaceful domesticity of our nature were required to produce untiring and honest officials for all these petty states. Men whose ambitions are directed towards great things, towards splendor and power, men different from us, would not have borne this misery—which only later appeared to be misery in our eyes and which even today is regarded by many as our greatest pride. Even though in these petty states the quiet detailed work of the official flourished most of all, even though burghers and peasants felt comfortable in the narrowest and most indigent circle, and even though idealism was not prevented from constructing the most magnificent castles in the air, it was nonetheless altogether impossible for these phantom states to aid in the development of real political life.

But it should not be forgotten that our primary concern was to acquire the first elements of a political education. After an absolutely unpolitical past of centuries, our primary concern was to take the first step from an existence entirely fulfilled by private interests and by domestic, scientific, poetic, and religious endeavours to the stage of political life. This step could be taken successfully only if the most distinguished minds of the nation participated most enthusiastically and only if great objectives beckoned them from their books and out of their homes to the market place. However, where in God's name did the German petty states present such goals and such circumstances during those years? Everything conspired to discourage even the political enthusiasts. And even if we had had men, endowed by nature with the greatest talents for successful political activity, they would have been deterred from pursuing a political career because of the utter impossibility of achieving satisfactory results or of even practicing these talents.

And so it happened that among the great numbers of distinguished scholars, artists, industrialists, judges, and officials whom Germany had produced in the thirty-three years following the establishment of the Confederation, few individuals can be mentioned to whom we can ascribe political importance. Many of the most important leaders of liberalism at that time stood intellectually far below the level to which men like Niebuhr and Savigny had raised our conception of the state. And even though on the whole their less sophisticated practice met the demands of the times more adequately than the wisdom of those conservatives, a more penetrating investigation clearly reveals that their opposition to the *Bundestag* arose from strongly particularistic motives. It also reveals that their liberalism did not hesitate, circumstances permitting, to disregard patriotic duty and national interest. One needs only to read Paul Pfizer's excellent correspondence between two Germans (1832) to realize how willing they were to promote constitutional interests with French help. One needs only to recall the strong opposition with which the *Zollverein* met in these liberal circles of the southwest to recognize the insecure and dubious basis which supported the beginnings of a free life. To be sure, each German chamber had its great representatives; to be sure, great men appeared here and there whose words echoed beyond the narrow borders of the land. There were even individuals whom the enthusiastic youth of the nation looked to with admiration. However, with a few exceptions, all these great men sank into the sweet sleep of oblivion after twenty or thirty years. Go into the various territories and inquire about the leaders of the opposition in 1820 or 1830. You will find only a few grateful people who have preserved a living memory of the patriotic deeds of those men who undertook to liberate their people from disgraceful conditions and who sacrificed a life filled with toil and self-denial for a cause which could not be achieved.

The abnormal attitude of our nobility was particularly responsible for the extreme difficulties with which this task met in every respect. In every monarchistic state the nobility is the truly political class. Not only has it been the case for centuries in England that the various classes of the nobility have almost exclusively borne the burden of political tasks, but also, on the continent, the nobility has without exception played a significant role in the affairs of state. The rather unsuccessful role of the nobility in the modern constitutional history of France and Spain is basically responsible for the small amount of progress which these countries have made to date in organized political freedom. On the other hand, Italy owes its unexpected success primarily to the intelligent and patriotic participation of its nobility in the great struggle for national rebirth.

The unalterable nature of circumstances is the reason for the following phenomenon which appears everywhere in the same manner: monarchic states have the choice either of achieving a modified constitution and parliamentary forms with the help of the nobility or of remaining under the rule of a bureaucratic and more or less absolute government. In all modern states the bourgeoisie became an important economic power and a proud authority of scientific and industrial intelligence. All modern states rest primarily on the work of the bourgeoisie; therefore, all modern states will have to grant the bourgeoisie an important role in political life. However, the middle class lacks the proper prerequisites for real political action. The middle class will always be a major factor in political life; its insight, its activity, and its wealth are above all demanded by the state. Its interests and inclinations will have to be considered foremost by every intelligent statesman. But the nature of its social position, the effect of its professional activity on lifelong habits, forms of character, and trends of thought will only in rare instances enable the middle-class man to work successfully in major political affairs. He will provide the chambers with the most prudent and knowledgeable members, but only seldom with leaders who are capable of mastering the entire situation with the grasp of a statesman, and of taking decisive action at the critical moment. He will provide the ministries with excellent advisers, but only seldom with ministers who are capable of associating as skillfully with the ruling masters as with the delegates. The burgher is cut out for work but not for command; and the essential task of the statesman is to rule.

The most able members of the bourgeoisie have worked themselves up from the bottom. Their cradles stood in narrow little rooms. In a limited and poor environment their youth was a struggle against all kinds of misery. Only later did they attain a position which allowed them a freer view of the world; work and toil for their family as a rule remains their lot until their creative energy is consumed. Such a life is most conducive to human competence. It builds character and freedom and purity of the soul. But he who worked his way up in this manner, is, so to speak, too good for politics. He has learned to trust his own strength in all things and to follow his own convictions; he does not yield or cringe; he bears within both a strong sense of masculine pride and humble modesty; he is strong, but awkward; he is conscientious, but stubborn. Place such a man into a circle of diplomats or place him beside a throne. In his heart he will look down upon them, and still he will be duped by them. The splendor of the castle will at times impress him too much and at times repulse him. He will always feel he is in a strange world, and he will yearn for the peace and independence of his bourgeois labor. Actually, at the core of its being the bourgeoise is democratic. This basic democratic feature will always place him in certain opposition to the aristocrats, who surround and support every monarch. This antagonism will have as its result that he either will act contrary to his nature and plunge into servile submission or will unprofitably expend a great deal of his best energy in constant friction.

But all these weaknesses are minor when compared to the fact that the bourgeois man entered politics rather late and from a totally different profession. He was not trained or educated to be a statesman, and he therefore lacked the knowledge, practice, and skills which are absolutely essential to the statesman. It is one of the most fatal errors, for which our totally unpolitical way of thinking and the lack of any important political experience are responsible, to believe that every conscientious scholar, lawyer, merchant, and official who is interested in public affairs and who diligently reads the newspaper is capable of actively engaging in politics. It is also one of our most fatal errors to believe that absolutely no specific preparation or education is required and that politics can be pursued successfully together with other professional duties. To be sure, if this kind of politics does not have greater objectives than to putter around with bills in some little chamber or to discharge a clerk here and a policeman there or to provide the constituency with a road or a railroad station, then intelligent burgomasters, officials, and judges under the direction of a somewhat more sagacious professor or lawyer would certainly comprise a very good council. However, no one will maintain that anything of significance will be accomplished with this kind of parliamentary activity. And as happens in even the smallest German chamber, decisions have to be made which require more than the mediocre knowledge of a constituency or the insight of a provincial philistine; more than the integrity of a dependent official. What would happen then? I know of no more curious sight than the one presented by our German chambers when they have to solve real political problems. The serious, conscientious, and thorough German people appear in those persons —whom they have entrusted with the power to decide their most important problems—in a manner which contrasts most unfavorably with their true nature. The men who sit on the green or red benches in those important moments are certainly recognized for their professional ability. How would they have otherwise won the confidence of the voters? But now they are supposed to decide issues which lie outside their range of vision—about which they can form no independent judgment and of which they have no thorough knowledge. They will either become the prey of ministerial superiority—which often forces them by the most obvious tricks to pass resolutions of whose consequences they are unaware; or they will be courageous enough to vote in opposition. This, however, has no practical results because the opposition only rarely has men at its disposal who would be in a position to take over the government. These men, however, are wanting because the assembly—with disappearing exceptions—is composed of persons who engage in politics only by the way. A chamber whose parties are not led by true statesmen is a monstrosity; statesmen, however—just as competent physicians, lawyers, and philologists—are not created overnight. Statesmen do not emerge from a dilettantish occupation in the state, but from earnest life-long service to the state. Politics is a profession, just as jurisprudence and medicine. It is the most noble and difficult profession to which a man can dedicate himself. It is a real offence against the German nation and the German name that we, who pursue the smallest things with the thorough concentration of all our energy, believe we can dispose of the greatest and noblest human matters, the affairs of state, with a playful dilettantism—we, who of all nations have to solve the most difficult political task with the most modest political talents.

If, however, important political achievements can be expected only from men who pursue politics as a life's profession, and if the middle class is not suited for a truly political career, it follows that the assistance of the nobility is essential to every people if it wants to solve great political tasks. We ourselves, among whom bourgeois character, views, and aspirations have attained undue predominance, have learned in our provincial life that the few truly outstanding political minds as a rule are members of the nobility! . . .

* * *

Only under the condition that the bourgeoisie send its best representatives into the real political class can the bourgeoisie leave the supreme command of the state to the nobility. And only upon the prudent partnership of interests among the various elements of the political community can a powerful state rest. The exact opposite of this normal relationship was true of Germany. Consequently our political development followed the most unpleasant path.

Nowhere in Europe except in Germany has the nobility long been the ally of absolutism; nowhere except in Germany has the nobility systematically advocated bureaucratic forms of government as opposed to the demand for self-government in which an important role falls to the nobility —whereas it is powerless next to the bureaucracy with all its courtly and military connections. This absurd attitude of our nobility completely poisoned the political struggles of liberalism in the small states, for it deprived liberalism of its natural leaders. In addition to the absolutist pressures of the two great powers, the attitude of the nobility was a further factor in sentencing liberalism to the role of unfruitful opposition. This attitude of the nobility finally gave liberalism a radical tendency, which became dangerous perhaps for the monarchy, but certainly for liberalism. . . .

* * *

In all military questions liberal opinion had submitted to rather radical views. There was a series of factors which made it possible to anticipate the opposition of public opinion to any increase of the military burden: a peace of almost fifty years, the dissatisfaction with the high and, as it appeared, superfluous expenditure for standing armies, the tempting example of Switzerland and the United States, the deceiving memory of the great achievements of the *Landwehr* from 1813 to 1815, hostility towards the absolutist tendencies of the military aristocracy, and an abhorrence in general of all the disturbances caused by war—which was only too natural at a time when industrialism continued to rise to ascendancy. It was quite obvious that for precisely these reasons only a liberal administration had a chance of obtaining the consent of the territorial representatives for such a reorganization. However, it was equally certain that liberal ministers could hope to solve this problem successfully only if they simultaneously removed all suspicion from liberalism in the eyes of the people and persuaded or assured them that additional expenditures in the military budget would be offset by the abolition of other burdens and obstacles, under whose pressure the country had suffered for many years. Precisely this reciprocal relationship presented the most valuable chance for the liberal system.

Those individuals and classes to whom the military reform was a matter of the greatest consequence for their particular proclivities and interests, at the same time caused the liberalism of the ministry the greatest difficulties. Thus the ministers found themselves in the unique position of having to relate the military question to the entire political problem, of having to court the one through the favor of the other and of having to join their assistance to the one with the desired concessions for the other. In January of 1860 Mr. von Manteuffel made the absolutely correct observation: If the Liberals were clever, they would oust us from office forever by means of the military problem.

At this first great opportunity to secure a firm and lasting liberal policy for the Prussian state, the Liberals evidenced a fatal lack of skill. Even before the public had received any details of the intended reorganization, the sudden resignation of the popular minister of war, von Bonin, became a bad omen for the further development of the matter. In general, von Bonin was considered to be a liberal military man. Of course, it was assumed that he had resigned because the reorganization of the army was to take place along reactionary lines, but in fact, completely different motives led to the minister's resignation. In reality, he would hardly have been equal to the problem which had to be solved. But the manner in which his resignation came about—without appropriate interest on the part of the other ministers —indicated that they had not known how to adopt the correct attitude with regard to a question which involved the existence of the entire government. Neither did they appear to have this attitude during the futher formulation of the proposal. Obviously it was not sufficient that they had obtained approval from the regent for a series of beneficial bills. They had to demand the guarantee that these bills would actually become law and would not be killed by the powerful influences in the ministries of the previous regime; in the highest posts of the provincial administration; in the *Herrenhaus;* and in the entourage of the prince himself.

Although the mood of the country in the last months had regrettably soured because of several events—for example the Schiller festival—nothing major was actually required to restore public confidence. It was not a question of translating bold experiments into legislation or of mercilessly purifying all the personnel. If the ministry had actually abolished some of the most oppressive abnormalities of the previous situation, if it had given evidence of its seriousness by discharging some of the officials who were hated with good reason, and if it had, above all, created in the *Herrenhaus* the necessary support for its policies, it cannot be doubted that the country would have agreed to accept a considerable increase in the financial burden. Above all, it was not of utmost importance to come to grips with the somewhat dull judgment of public opinion, but rather to come to an agreement with the leaders of the Chamber of Deputies and with the party members of long standing, one which excluded any unfounded suspicion from either side.

The party to which the majority of the ministers belonged now formed the overwhelming majority in the Chamber of Deputies. It would not now be difficult to convince the most respected members of the majority of the necessity of the military reform. They needed only to be informed of the entire situation. Nor would it be difficult to win their support—even if it were not immediately possible to offer the Chamber of Deputies the entire sum of constitutional guarantees in return. Such an open and frank exchange between the ministers and their very influential friends in the Chamber of Deputies could also make up for the serious difficulties in the ministerial position.

I do not believe it can be said that exaggerated demands of an ideal policy have been developed in the above paragraphs. They contained only what was absolutely obvious and essential. On the other hand, if one points out the great difficulties which the ministers encountered in pursuing this policy, one would have to reply that great problems are always bound up with great difficulties. Indeed, we were dealing with something great. It was a question of leading Prussia from the wrong path of revolutionary and counterrevolutionary excesses back to the secure path of sound and constantly progressive politics. It was a question of giving the German problem a beneficial turn through a strong Prussia and of reviving through a Prussia backed up by Germany the old order of Europe, which was visibly out of joint, in a way demanded by the interests of Prussia and Germany and of civilization in general. No instance could be thought of which had offered true statecraft more propitious circumstances. In Prussia, in Germany, and in Europe the most dynamic elements lay scattered. A policy with a goal in mind could set these elements in motion for its own purposes. In Prussia and Germany everyone longed for a power which knew how to sever itself only somewhat favorably well from the gloomy past. To be certain, the European situation held dangers; but it also presented the unique opportunity for raising Prussia from forty years of insignificance to a position of appropriate influence.

*   *   *

In the January (1860) issue of the Prussian annuals I drew special attention to the following point: "In review of the sad events of the previous year it was stated that their experiences should really stimulate us to think seriously about ourselves! For, whatever we might say, each of us was partly to blame. For almost a decade we all, with a few exceptions, had postponed the essential political work, which, to be sure, was a difficult and thankless task. Everybody was more concerned with his private affairs and more or less forgot the issues common to all. Eleven years ago we set about like dilettantes pursuing the rich pleasures of an interesting public life; we quickly outdid ourselves. When the fruits of politics became bitter, most of the people became disgusted, and they returned to their comfortable private libraries and their offices. When the storm which had suddenly gathered called us back to public life, we had on the whole learned little and forgotten much. Public duties cannot be undertaken in such a sporadic fashion. Like any other kind of learning or art, politics requires loyal devotion and serious energy. And if it appeals little to our customs and inclinations to devote our best energy to restless and thankless activity in the market place of public life, nonetheless reason should aid us in recognizing that it is impossible for us to overcome the particularly great difficulties of satisfactorily organizing the German state. If a respectable number of gifted men does not dedicate itself to the Fatherland, reason should help us to recognize that all our erudition, education, and prosperity are built upon sand, as long as the foundation of everything—a sound state—is lacking."

* * *

Hitherto we Germans have squandered so much valuable energy largely because this political way of thinking is extremely alien to our nature. We are students of theory, who make a judgment about things completely independent of all circumstances. We are children of a religious past, and religion does not question the circumstances. We have grown up in a quiet home where firm virtue is justifiably more important than cautious shrewdness. Even where our activity approaches political practice, we prefer to follow the letter of the law or instruction rather than an independent conception of the circumstances. Whoever is guided by the latter is quickly reproached for arbitrary action. In politics, however, this purely pertinent settlement of business leads to the worst blunders. This manner of settling affairs is customary in our chambers. It was followed by the liberals in the Prussian Chamber of Deputies in the fatal session of 1860.

* * *

By a bold offensive Prussia rose, grew, and was delivered from the misery of 1807. Because of the circumstances this offensive became Prussia's natural law. It could not remain what it was. It had to become very great or small again. The destiny of Prussia and of Germany could be fulfilled only if the borders of Prussian power were extended to those of Germany. Only in Germany could the strength be found which would secure Prussia's existence, if it had no European alliance. Only Germany could give Prussia the supplement, which it could not dispense with, if it were to transfer the overwrought state of its financial and military resources—which in the long run would have been intolerable—to a normal effort. The national uprising of Italy aroused of necessity similar efforts in Germany. . . . And what was the result? The states of secondary importance gathered in Würzburg and drafted a great conspiracy against Prussia. They rejected the proposals for the reform of the Confederate military organization, which by far did not meet the demands established by Prussia. They attempted to draw maritime affairs into the sphere of the Confederacy. In the question of Electoral Hesse they adhered to the old oppression. Mr. von Borries disclosed the intrinsic meaning of this coalition with the notorious words of May 1st: that the German princes would prefer to call for the help of foreign states rather than recognize the leading position of Prussia. And as people in various parts of Germany expressed their indignation at this manifestation of patriotism in those states, the King of Hanover confirmed the dictum of his minister by elevating him to earldom.

Lay not a serious danger for Prussia in those circumstances? Could even at that time an unbiased observer doubt that this German chaos could only be ordered, if either the Prussian sword were unsheathed or if it were at least to threaten the petty kings with considerable heat. Or if one had perchance the proper patience to let the German question completely rest for some time, it would have been impossible for one to have the patience not to requisition a certain part of German strength for the European position of Prussia. However, one could depend upon this only if Prussian military power stood alert and prepared for a strong offensive attack, only if Prussia cast off the bonds of a military organization directed totally towards defense, and only if it were in a position to calmly confront alone a bellicose threat by a major European power. Prussia did not have to fear the intrigues of its royal neighbors only if they trembled before its power.

*   *   *

A political way of thinking had to come to the conclusion that the acceptance of the military bill was unavoidable. In spite of everything a political manner of dealing with the question had to have considerable support, which would allow the acceptance of the military bill to appear not merely as a difficult sacrifice. The Chamber of Deputies had the power to place the European and German questions in the foreground in such a way that even superficial liberalism would automatically learn to view military affairs in a different manner. Of course, precisely in this point of foreign politics the Liberal Party suffered from a serious lack of fundamental knowledge and rich experience. Hardly any members of the liberal party had ever exercised practical activity in this field; least of all from books can one obtain useful information in the practical aspects of politics. However, even that which literature offered in this respect was unknown to many. Foreign politics had lain almost totally outside the range of even the Prussian liberals. This was a natural result of the fact that since 1815 Prussia had no foreign policy worth mentioning. In general, the Chamber of Deputies had to discard the fetters which bound it to small details and to the limitations of bureaucratic diligence in the commissions. It had to pursue politics. It had to impress opponents and support friends in the ministry, and it had to guide public opinion instead of being guided by it. Had the ministers in the palace not taken the proper stand, then there were individual delegates who could have corrected this error. Perhaps these were nothing but demands which exceeded the usual range of accomplishments. But was not something crucial at stake? Was it worthy of serious men to allow an extremely important attempt to fail before the last bit of energy had been expended?

However, we unfortunately take a different attitude toward political tasks than we do to all others. We look down upon the man who in scientific or industrial affairs shrinks from being completely serious. For us it is understood that business of a private nature, where great decisions are involved, must be pursued with complete dedication. On the other hand, a defeat in public affairs is nothing disgraceful to us. In public affairs acquiescence is understood among us. These affairs lay almost beyond our feeling of duty. They hardly touch our innermost sentiments. For us they do not form an existential problem.

With this resignation the Chamber of Deputies also set about the problem of the army. The circumstances were simply accepted as given. The ministers, the crown, the *Herrenhaus,* the press, and public opinion had fashioned the situation in such a way that the approval of the new military budget appeared to be impossible. It would have been a question of improving this situation with creative energy. People accepted the situation as a misfortune which had to be tolerated. People suffered instead of acting. And finally a compromise was reached which became the source of the most vexing quarrels. To agree to the military reform as provisional readiness for war was certainly a thought which attested to the active wish for settlement, as well as to the hopeless confusion of the situation.

The Liberal Party had failed just as had the liberal ministry. The fact that the liberal system was able to stay in power for another two years seems to indicate that this system would have had a great opportunity if it had taken a different attitude toward the affairs of government. I believe that not only the country but also the ruler vigorously maintained the position he had chosen when he assumed power, and that it was difficult for him to personally alter the system. But after the session of 1860 it was almost impossible to entertain any hope for the policies of the new era. The necessary understanding between the government and public opinion, between public opinion and the Chamber of Deputies, had been too thoroughly shattered.

4 The Historians' Views

*Guido de Ruggiero's study of liberalism is a classic. In the
selection that follows he examines the factors in Germany
that led to the conflict between liberalism and nationalism.*

FROM The History of European Liberalism in the Nineteenth Century BY GUIDO DE RUGGIERO

HEGEL'S DOCTRINE is a theoretical synthesis of two opposed German
tendencies struggling for predominance in the first half of the nineteenth
century. In the field of militant politics their effective reconciliation, so far at
least as concerns the fundamentals of public law, had to wait till a much later
date.

Prussian Liberalism, which flourished after Jena, made its last appear-
ance in the customs law of 1818, conceived according to the principle of free
trade and containing only in a minor degree measures of retaliation against
the protectionism of other nations; implicitly against that of England, which
in 1815 had limited the importation of grain. In a country which was
essentially an exporter of agricultural produce and devoid of industry, as
Prussia was in 1815, this free trade was natural enough without appeal to the
feeling for liberty, which at this time had almost vanished from the governing classes. But the Liberal consequences of the law were important, because
it formed the centre round which all the other German States grouped
themselves into the Zollverein of 1833. Thus the consequences of liberty
survived the eclipse of the Liberal spirit in Prussia, and offer to political
history a striking proof of the importance of liberty as a means towards
national unification. Liberal opinion, widely diffused among the German
States of the west and south, extracted from the Zollverein a powerful motive

Guido de Ruggiero, *The History of European Liberalism*, pp. 241–51, translated by R. G.
Collingwood. Reprinted by permission of Beacon Press and The Clarendon Press, Oxford.
First published by the Oxford University Press in 1927. First published as a Beacon Paperback in
1959.

for a close union between the idea of freedom and that of the Fatherland, and for bringing pressure on Prussia to induce her to promote a general political movement towards liberty and to take the lead towards national unification.

But Prussia was now governed according to the ideals of the Holy Alliance, and disappointed all Liberal hopes. And the complications which Liberalism introduced into the national problem aggravated the Austrian government's inherent anti-Liberalism. Metternich realized that a Liberal Prussia would mean the end of the Austrian hegemony and of the Austro-Prussian equilibrium in the German federation; he therefore made every effort not only to arouse all Austrophil Germans against the Liberals, but also to encourage Frederick William III of Prussia in his policy of reaction. He regarded a monarchy tempered by representation of the feudal classes as the best government for Prussia; a view shared by the Prussian government, which in 1823 reorganized the provincial diets, redistributing them into three orders according to their territorial possessions, so as to give a safe majority to the landed aristocracy, the owners of the so-called *Rittergüter,* while the *bourgeois* not possessed of land, professional men, capitalists, and tradesmen, were entirely unrepresented.

The States of Southern Germany enjoyed a far more Liberal régime than that of Prussia. In most of them the constitutions of the period from 1814 to 1848 were modelled on the charter of Louis XVIII. The Liberal theories of these countries, too, much resembled the constitutionalism of Constant, Royer-Collard, and Daunou. They were represented in great part by university professors, the two Rottecks, Welcker, Friedrich Gagern, Jacob Grimm, Stockmar, Rümelin, Robert Mohl, Gervinus, and others. The programme of Carl Rotteck, the earliest of them, and therefore interesting as the original document of the school, is a defence of rational rights as against historic rights. By this Rotteck means a legal and political system directed to attaining the rational ends of man, and recognizing, in a Kantian spirit, the claim of every individual to a freedom compatible to that of the rest. In all these writers Liberal feeling is combined with national feeling, thus originating the movement of thought which was to have its epilogue in the parliament of Frankfurt.

But the first struggles of university Liberalism were conducted within the schools and by academic weapons. Only the extreme autonomy of the German universities could permit professors living in the centre of Europe, between a reactionary Prussia and a reactionary Austria, to expound Liberal ideas to their students. Thus when, owing to government pressure, the freedom of teaching was here and there violated, the universities became centres and hotbeds of revolt. The most famous example is the protest of the historian Dahlmann of Göttingen, which bore the signatures of the brothers Grimm, Gervinus, Eduard Albrecht, and others, against the Hanoverian government in 1837 on its violating the constitution it had sworn to respect. The protest was the more significant in that not only the liberty of the university but that of the country at large was at stake, and the professors felt the incompatibility of their function with the act of a government that failed to abide by its solemn pledges. "Must I," said Dahlmann and the court-counsellor Albrecht, "teach henceforward that the supreme principle of the State is that whatever pleases those in power is law? As a man of honour, I would cease to teach rather than sell to my audience for truth that which is a lie and a deceit."

The seven professors who signed the protest were expelled from their chairs; but the people of Göttingen, mindful of the Liberalism which they had learnt to value under English government, opened a public subscription on their behalf. And the defences of their conduct written after their reappointment by Dahlmann and Jacob Grimm are rightly regarded by Germans as the loftiest examples of their own Liberal literature. In them the peculiar *forma mentis* of German Liberalism stands out, in contrast not only with an arbitrary absolutism, but also with the anti-historical rationalism dear to the Liberal extremists most influenced by France. Thus Dahlmann denies the right of the people to take the law into its own hands; and Grimm, answering those Liberals who despised the barbarism of the Middle Ages, does not conceal his deep sympathy for the ancient medieval liberties of the people, and his delight in slaking his thirst at the far-off springs of German life.

The greatest obstacle to the success of the national Liberal programme was the attitude of Prussia. Frederick William IV, coming to the throne in 1840, carried yet farther the reactionary tendencies of his predecessor. He was a belated Romantic, moved by the contradictory desires for a revived medievalism and a legitimatistic assertion of the divine right of kings. The great development of the *bourgeoisie* during the twenty years of his reign took place unobserved beneath his very eyes. Surrounded by a little clique of catholicizing Romantics, he devoted his political energies to a revival of the old feudal classes, and on the very eve of the Revolution of 1848 set about altering his predecessor's constitution by erecting a House of Lords above the representatives of the three classes, as if to accentuate a class distinction in order to impress the *bourgeoisie*. In convoking the new diet, he insisted on the special position of his State between the three Great Powers, by ordaining which "it pleases God to make Prussia great by means of the sword, the sword of war without, the sword of the spirit within; not the negative spirit of our age, but the spirit of discipline and order." He added:

> No power on earth shall ever persuade me to exchange the natural relation between prince and people for a contractual and constitutional relation; or to countenance the insertion, between our Lord in Heaven and this country, of a piece of written paper, like a second providence, to rule by its paragraphs and to take the place of ancient sacred loyalty.

The increasing rigidity of Prussia in her traditional attitude formed a serious obstacle to the execution of the Liberal programme of a national unification by means of liberty, and split the party into two camps. The more moderate Liberals continued to hope for a change of heart on the part of Prussia, in the sense that if the king saw an opportunity to make a bid for the crown of all Germany, a feeling for his own dynastic interests might induce him to form a *mariage de convenance* with freedom; the more radical Liberals began to look for a unification in spite of Prussia, at the price of the absorption of the Prussian kingdom in a Liberal Germany.

But in Prussia the same politicians who were farthest from the romantic spirit of the king, and shared with the Liberals a hope of national unification, recoiled from this extreme of radicalism. In their opinion the hegemony of an armed Prussia was the only guarantee for true unity, the only force capable of permanently uniting the numerous petty States of Germany, overcoming their anarchical particularism and arousing their dormant political feeling. Thus to the Liberal idea of a federation of autonomous sovereign States (*Staatenbund*) they opposed the idea of a federal State (*Bundesstaat*) with Prussia as its centre. The reactionary policy of Frederick William IV they regarded as an antiquated and out-of-date, but none the less providential, method of resisting the disintegrating forces of Liberalism, and saving the Prussian State in its existing form for its future task.

Thus the medievalism of the king became the vehicle of a highly modern imperialistic conception of the nation, in contrast with the Liberal conception. The realization of this change is the clearest proof of the profound historical sense of Ranke, Droysen, and Sybel, and of the political astuteness shown by Bismarck in his role of reactionary during the Revolution of 1848.

For these politicians the national idea was an inference from historical premises resembling those of Romanticism; but far from exhausting itself in a sterile reminiscence and passive admiration of the past, it brought its forces, drawn from the tradition of centuries, to bear upon the present and point towards the future, towards the expansion and domination of the German people. Not the nation as a vague sentimental entity, but the nation as an instrument of power, was the object of their love and, still more, of their political activity. They did not reject the nation of the Romantics; they wished to use its conservative energies, its archaic but solid structure, its narrow but powerful monarchy, as a platform on which to construct the new Germany. They took up the cause of Prussia not out of love of the old feudal Prussia, but because a strong Prussia could give to all Germany the form of a State, and enable it to take a place in the great international competition. Unlike their allies or tools, the pure reactionaries, they did not ignore the importance of the rapidly rising *bourgeoisie,* but wished to wean it from the philistinic ideals of a barren individualism, indoctrinate it with their own conceptions, and convert it into a progressive force to operate upon the sluggish landed aristocracy. While English and French Liberalism tended to shape the nation upon the mould of middle-class economic life, they proposed to mould this economic life to the needs of the nation, combining it with pre-existent and even outworn forces in such a way that each class should make its contribution to the common cause.

This was the motive of their protectionism, formulated for the first time, and with full consciousness of its national end, by Friedrich List in his *National System of Political Economy* in 1841. In this system the author's opposition to competition and *laissez-faire* is based not upon the social and humanitarian motives of the French and English Conservatives, nor upon the purely technical motives of Utopian Socialism, but on a totally different order of ideas. The aim of free competition, according to the classical school, was to increase the present wealth available for national consumption; the predominant consideration was that of value in exchange. List, on the other hand, introduced into the discussion two new ideas: the idea of nationality, as opposed to that of international free trade, and the idea of productive power, as opposed to that of exchange value. As against cosmopolitanism, he showed that individual prosperity closely depends upon the political power of the nation. As against the idea that productive activity ought to tend towards the creation of the maximum quantity of exchangeable values, he asserted the necessity of safeguarding the sources of labour and economic life, and ensuring the future development of these energies, on the ground that the power to create riches is infinitely more important than riches themselves.

Now according to the theory of free trade, it cannot pay a nation to create an industry when, as was the case with Germany about the year 1840, it can purchase the industrial products which it needs cheaper in foreign countries, in exchange for agricultural products which it can produce more cheaply. But this narrowly utilitarian calculation would, according to List, deprive the nation of its best energies. Industry best develops the moral energies of a people. The desire for a constant increase of intellectual and moral goods, the love of emulation and liberty, is characteristic of an industrial and commercial state; under the régime of a uniform agriculture, dullness of mind, sloth of body, and attachment to old ideas and habits are the rule. Even agriculture is powerfully stimulated by the presence of manufactures. The State, therefore, by suitable legislation must encourage the birth and growth of industries.

Here economics are clearly subordinated to national organization. But not economics only; all the other energies of the people are to be treated in the same way. Freedom also, with its autonomous institutions, is a source of national energy; and the arguments which we have reproduced led List to distinguish clearly between the cause of protection and that of anti-Liberalism. Indeed, in the rise of industry, even under protection, he saw a means of a liberal education for the people. But freedom, like industry, like agriculture, like intellectual culture, has the value of a mere means to a higher national end. In a spirit not unlike that of List, Bismarck, the reactionary of 1848, later granted the nation universal suffrage when he came to see in this a useful means of consolidating the Empire; he was willing either to form an alliance with the Liberal Party or to set on foot the *Kulturkampf,* whose anti-Liberal character is obvious.

The danger of this tendency to subordinate and sacrifice every value to the idol of nationality is that the spirit of the people may lose its sense of direction, and that stability and firmness may disappear from the current of public opinion through the prevalence of the idea that these values are contingent and accidental; and in minds of a lower order, less strongly sustained by the consciousness of the higher end, this means degeneration into a cynical opportunism. The nationalism of Bismarck, Droysen, and Treitschke failed to create a true governing class, because it was too much of an original work of art, requiring for its perfection a lofty intellect capable of mastering a recalcitrant and uninspiring matter. Now a political tradition cannot base its continuity upon a succession of great men. Bismarck could only create lieutenants; and when he vanished from the political stage, the technical and administrative subordinates who had worked under him in a complex and highly organized machine showed themselves unable to perform a task of synthesis for which they had not been trained.

Another danger of this form of nationalism is that by turning the nation into a weapon of aggression and conquest it threatens to destroy the basis on which the idea of the nation, and therefore the possibility of the coexistence of different nations, is built. The imperialism which inevitably proceeds from such a tendency not only claims the right of enslaving weaker nations, but runs the risk of corrupting the spirit of the conquering nation, by disintegrating its forces into a super-State composed of heterogeneous elements whose artificial cohesion demands a diversion of these forces from their normal function in the historical life of the nation. While the reactionary nationalism of the Romantics sacrificed the future of the national life to the love of the past, the new imperialism, which was not unconnected with its predecessor, sacrificed to ambitious hopes for the future the traditional historic character of the German people.

At this point the fundamental contrast between this conception and the political idea of the nation becomes clear. The one considers the nation only as an element in the power of the State; the other erects it into an independent value superior to the State, enclosing and entrenching the latter within the inviolable limits of the nation. Thus for Liberalism the peaceful coexistence of a number of nations, each organized as a State and conducting its relations with its neighbours on the same principles that govern the relations of free and self-conscious individuals, is a necessary condition of political stability and progress. From this point of view it is possible to appreciate the great difference between the national claims of most European peoples during the nineteenth century, directed to the achievement, through revolution and war, of a work of emancipation, and the projects of expansion and hegemony inspired by the spirit of an imperialistic nationalism.

The great campaign of German Liberalism for national unity was fought in 1848. The Liberals put forward three closely connected proposals:

to liberate the German States from the paternalism of Austria; to obtain, especially in Prussia, genuinely modern constitutions in place of the old feudal diets; and to make these constitutions a bond of political union for the whole German people.

The first of these proposals could be carried out easily and almost instantaneously. Austria, weakened by a revolutionary crisis at home, a war against Italy, and a rebellion in Hungary, could offer little resistance to the German federation in its struggle for freedom. The weakness of Austria resulted in the paralysis of the pro-Austrian party, which called itself the Great German Party, and proposed to include the Austrian nation in a Greater Germany. This party, in a small minority at the parliament of Frankfurt, disappeared from the scene together with its patroness Austria, and the partisans of a smaller Germany remained masters of the field.

The second point in the Liberal programme was won at the first attack by the *bourgeois* revolution, which wrested from the terrified rulers the constitutional concessions that had long been demanded. This revolution was particularly violent in Prussia, where the monarchical reaction had been most energetic. Unlike the contemporary revolution in France, it had no marked social character, because industry had not yet developed in Prussia, and the agricultural masses were still in a backward state of feudal civilization which prevented their infection by the revolutionary feeling of the lesser *bourgeoisie*. The soul of the revolution was the city *bourgeoisie,* led by professors and students, the educated classes among which the claims of Liberalism had been longer felt and more vividly realized. But absolutism, defeated in the towns, was uninjured and ready for the counter-attack in the country, the stronghold of feudalism. Bismarck gives in his *Memoirs* an interesting picture of this state of mind, which he expounded to the king in order to engage him on the side of reaction. But Frederick William no longer needed such aids. In the army, a force of feudal origin so far as officers and men were concerned, but educated in the school of monarchy, he possessed the quintessence of the forces of ancient and modern Prussia; and once the first period of dismay was over he employed this powerful weapon to put down the revolution.

The third task of the German Liberals was more complicated. It was taken in hand under the happy auspices of the revolutionary victory in Prussia, which favoured the hope of a unification of Germany with a Liberal Prussia at its head. It expressed an ideal towards which no party, even the most reactionary, could display a *fin de non-reçevoir.* Yet this ideal was opposed by the best representatives of culture and politics, who, as we have seen, were partisans of a new nationalism. These agreed in desiring unification, but not by an act of popular sovereignty, which would create a weak State, at the mercy of parties, and condemn Prussia to a secondary position where she could make no use of her actual military superiority. Hence we find an alliance in common opposition to the Liberal programme taking shape, between the old conservative classes, anxious for internal reaction, and the most modern representatives of imperialism, ready to use the former's power of resistance in order to oppose the revolutionary project of a federation of German States. The ancient alliance between the monarchy and the feudal nobility was reasserted and confirmed.

And while the conservative classes seconded the efforts of "King Grapeshot" (as the King of Prussia was nicknamed) to suppress the Liberal revolution, the nationalists criticized and ridiculed the debates in the parliament of Frankfurt, which, intended to settle the question of national unity, were gradually degenerating into empty verbal disputes as the people's representatives lost their prestige beneath the rising tide of reaction, and found themselves impotent to obtain any practical sanction for their resolutions. Nationalist historians have described the Frankfurt sessions as shining examples of doctrinaire abstraction and practical ineffectiveness. Partisan passions have prevented them from coolly realizing the exceptional conditions under which the representatives of the people were compelled to work, fettered by the heavy diplomatic yoke of two Great Powers, and, even more serious, hampered in carrying out their mandate by a permanent conflict between the sovereignty of parliament and that of the confederated States in whose hands any final decision must lie. But for the nationalists, the manifest impotence of the parliament was enough to discredit popular assemblies as such, and to create in the public mind a sense of distrust towards the futile and abstract sham-politics of professors and lawyers. The example of Frankfurt, aggravated by the historians' misrepresentations, was fatal to German political Liberalism. The people lost all interest in representative institutions, and made up its mind, to its own loss, that its political future depended wholly upon the Crown.

The closing scenes of the Frankfurt parliament, by a fiasco striking enough to impress itself permanently on the memory of the people, crowned the work of the doctrinaire impotence displayed by the representatives during the whole session. In the sitting of the 28th of March 1849, the assembly, after settling the internal crisis between the Prussian and Austrian parties in favour of the former, in spite of the Prussian reaction then in full swing, elected Frederick William IV Emperor of the Germans by 290 votes, 248 abstaining. But the King of Prussia refused the crown offered him by the representatives of the people, and explained in private why he had done so: the crown which a Hohenzollern could accept, he said, was not a crown created, even with the consent of princes, by a revolutionary assembly. If the ancient crown of the German nation, he added, which for forty-two years had lain idle, was to be conferred upon any one, it ought to have been conferred by himself and his equals, the other princes.

The king's haughty legitimism was a generation behind the times; but in its effects, if not in its motives, it harmonized admirably with the views of the most advanced politicians, who regarded unification as a problem of sheer force, to be solved by the sword. History has shown that both the king and politicians were right; for the Empire was created by the military

strength of the Hohenzollerns, combined with the *Realpolitik* of the nationalists, to the complete exclusion of any expression of popular consent, or
any aid from the spirit of an "antiquated" Liberalism. Yet the Liberal sense
of nationality, outwardly ignored, never ceased to live and work silently in
the depths of the popular mind; and in the darkest hour of the Empire,
when the force which was to be its only effectual bond had failed, the nation
was able to maintain its unity as a State in virtue of a right based on purely
Liberal principles, and thus to feel itself still firmly united in spite of threats
of internal disruption. The representatives united at Weimar at last did
justice to the Utopian generosity of Frankfurt.

> *Hans Kohn of the City College of New York is one of the
> foremost modern students of nationalism and its conse-
> quences in the modern world.*

FROM *The Mind of Germany* BY HANS KOHN

HEINRICH HEINE DIED IN 1856—in the midst of a profound change
in the political and moral climate of Germany. As late as 1840 liberals were
influencing major decisions, but by 1870 most of the liberals had turned into
nationalists. To the historian Friedrich Sell this was a tragedy. Tragic indeed
were the consequences, but the word *tragedy* is misleading, for it implies that
the German liberals were unwittingly tangled in events outside their control.
The truth is that most liberals were convinced that they had to choose
between a free society and a unified power state. Wittingly and willingly
they preferred national power to individual liberty.

The turning point meant a break not only with the West but also with
most of Germany's past. For Goethe the small town and principality of
Weimar set the stage for a wide-open world of cultural intercourse and for
the intensity of fruitful daily work. For the generation of 1870 the Prussian
power-state alone seemed to guarantee a worthwhile national and personal
life. Goethe as we have seen had no use for the Middle Ages. Now the
Prussian dynasty of the Hohenzollern was greeted as the legitimate successor
of the Hohenstaufen.

The interest in their empire was revived in the 1820's by a number of
historical and poetical works. Friedrich von Raumer, Professor at the Uni-

Reprinted with the permission of Charles Scribner's Sons and Macmillan & Co. Ltd., London,
from *The Mind of Germany: The Education of a Nation*, pp. 128–35, 137–41, and 143, by Hans
Kohn. Copyright © 1960 Hans Kohn.

versity of Berlin, began publication in 1823 of a six-volume "History of the Hohenstaufen and their Times." It presented the Hohenstaufen Reich not only as the first European power of its times, but also as a much more centralized national state than was actually the case. Under the influence of Raumer's widely read work, Karl Leberecht Immermann wrote a tragedy, "Kaiser Friedrich II," in 1828, and Ernst Benjamin Raupach wrote a cycle of not less than sixteen plays called "Die Hohenstaufen," which in spite of the fact that today his name has long been forgotten, were very popular in their day, so popular that in 1832 young Richard Wagner wrote an overture on this subject. More talented than Raupach was Christian Dietrich Grabbe; his two plays on the same subject may be read even today. In 1849 Raumer was a member of the delegation which on behalf of the German National Assembly offered the imperial crown to the Hohenzollern King. He lived long enough to witness, as a nonagenarian in 1871, the assumption by the Hohenzollern of the imperial title which popular imagination confounded with that of the Hohenstaufen. But the two had nothing in common. The Hohenstaufen Reich was rooted in southern Germany; in its religion it was Catholic; in its concept it was universal; and many of the Hohenstaufen felt more Mediterranean than German.

In the mid-nineteenth century the Prussian historian, Heinrich von Sybel, proposed a new interpretation of German history, which, under the impact of the Prussian victories was soon generally accepted. The new interpretation shifted the center of German history to the northeast, made Protestantism its dominant and creative religion, and based this religion upon a strictly nation-centered concept. Its outlook was not only anti-Roman and anti-Mediterranean, but antiwestern. It saw German history after the fall of the Hohenstaufen reaching its first climax in the War of Liberation fought under Prussia's leadership against France, and finding its fulfillment in Prussia's victory over France in 1871.

Such were the forces that brought about the close co-operation of most German liberal intellectuals with the Prussian authoritarian monarchy. The co-operation was originally not sought by either of the two sides. They neither loved nor trusted each other. But Prussia, which had little liking for modern liberalism, seemed the only country to offer what so many liberals desired, power to achieve national greatness and to restore Germany, as in the time of the Hohenstaufen, to the imperial leadership in Europe. In the end, after some resistance, but not too unwillingly or ungraciously, most liberals capitulated to Prussia. In return, the latter made minor concessions to the liberals, concessions without which a modern power-state could not have existed but which did not go far enough to transform Prussia into a durable and viable modern society.

There was nothing traditional or hallowed about the Prussian monarchy. The kingdom came into existence on January 18, 1701, when the Elector of Brandenburg assumed the title of king in Prussia. This took place in Königsberg, a city in the extreme northeast of Germany, then politically and spiritually outside Germany proper. It was a German outpost surrounded on all sides by Slav and Lithuanian populations which had been subjugated in the late Middle Ages by the Teutonic Knights. From its original domain, the March of Brandenburg, itself a frontier territory occupying former Slav lands east of the Elbe River, the power of the House of Hohenzollern had spread over many territorially disconnected possessions, which were united only by two factors: the dynasty and the need of defending long frontiers in a shapeless plain, a landscape much more characteristic of eastern than of western Europe. From the end of the seventeenth century Brandenburg, until then a minor German state, was bent upon glory and expansion. It lacked natural resources and its soil was poor; thus, it could achieve military strength only by the most efficient and economical administration and by giving full precedence to the military.

Life in eighteenth century Prussia was dominated by a stern sense of duty and service, by frugality and cultural insensibility. The emphasis was on efficiency, self-reliance, and thrift, not, as in the middle-class world of puritanism, for the sake of the individual and of religion but for the sake of the authoritarian state and of military power. Its own historians praised the Prussian state as the personification of political power. The state became the fountainhead of ethical life and the center of devotion.

In the eighteenth century Prussia was alien to the German mind and suspect to the German intellectuals who hated its garrison-spirit. The princes who founded Prussian greatness in that century, the dedicated soldier-king Frederick William I and his more complex and famous son Frederick II, had no regard or understanding for German cultural life. Prussia owed little to Germany and gave little. Its astonishing growth was dominated by only one goal—power—and only one norm—Prussia.

During the Napoleonic period a generation of great reformers, almost all of them born outside Prussia, tried to infuse Prussian power with a German spirit and to liberalize the monarchy. Their efforts saved Prussia and made victory in the war of 1813 possible. After that, reforms were halted. The University of Berlin, founded in 1810 as a part of the reform movement, became in many ways a model of scholarship and efficiency, but its professors accepted the authority of the state so willingly that one of the leading scholars there could call himself and his colleagues "the intellectual bodyguard of the Hohenzollern." This description was intended by the author and received by his colleagues as high praise. It was to this unreformed Prussia, the openly acknowledged bulwark of authoritarianism and conservative militarism, that most German liberals turned for guidance and inspiration.

This change in the attitude of the German liberals can best be followed in the writing of the German historians, from Johann Gustav Droysen, born in 1808, to Heinrich von Treitschke who died in 1896. Leopold von Ranke, whom they acknowledged as their master, belonged to an older generation.

He never was a liberal. Nevertheless, his political thought influenced many of those who called themselves liberal. "Ranke asserted the right of any state to follow its own logic of politics, its right to be different from the strict standard of liberalism," writes Professor Theodore H. von Laue in his study of Ranke's formative years. "The consequences of this assertion were momentous. It implied a break with the political development in France, England, and the United States. Under its guidance Prussia preserved the absolutist state of the eighteenth century instead of following the western trend toward democracy, and the more pacifist evaluation of international relations. The philosophy which Ranke so clearly stated was one of the landmarks in the revolt against the West, upholding against the advocates of western liberalism a new Prussophilism, which in time grew into a Germanophilism."

What separated Ranke from his successors was not merely his conservatism. Like Hegel, Ranke was no nationalist. He accepted the Europe of his time and believed in the concert of nations, whereas an historian like Droysen demanded the pre-eminence of the one nation clearly marked out for leadership. Ranke believed in the authoritarian monarchical state; Droysen believed in the German nation-state. Ranke still participated in the open world of Goethe, and in the balanced Europe of Metternich. Droysen finally embraced nothing except Germany and its national self-interest.

German historians and the German people ultimately accepted the idealization of state and power which Ranke held in common with Hegel, and as time went on oversimplified and vulgarized it. Perhaps the most generous judgment on Ranke's influence on nineteenth century German thought was expressed in 1886, on the occasion of Ranke's ninetieth birthday, by a Dutch historian, Robert Fruin, a master of the critical method himself and a liberal in the western sense of the word. "To us, who find more in the history of mankind than just the impact of power, and who care for other interests besides those of the State, Ranke's writings, however beautiful, will always appear lacking in something and unsatisfying. . . . Is it an injustice to our German neighbors to suggest that it is this characteristic attitude which has earned for Ranke the position of the historian *par excellence* of present-day Germany? Or is it not true that to the rulers and leaders of opinion in that country the power of the State is the overriding consideration? That to it everything else must give way and is, if need be, sacrificed? Prosperity, trade, and industry, are not promoted in accordance with their own needs and the laws of political economy, but are managed with an eye to the demands of State power, in the interests of the unity and efficiency of the Reich. Everything is regarded as lawful in these, and alas in other, respects, whenever German unity and German ascendancy in Europe might otherwise be thought to suffer."

*   *   *

Looking back to the War of Liberation, the liberals of this generation rejoiced in the recollection of the high moral standard maintained by the German people in their struggle against the French. Droysen's colleague Friedrich Christoph Dahlmann could not conceal his disgust for French frivolity when, in 1815, he came to deliver an academic address celebrating the victory over Napoleon. "Any one of us in the future who considers the French and the Germans merely as two hostile nations fighting with equal right on each side, any one of us who goes on believing that he would act in the same way if he were born a Frenchman, any one of us who compares this people who have so ignominiously degenerated, this rapacious people who commit perjury and deny God, with the noble and self-sacrificing Germans, he, wherever he be born, is really French and deserves so to be regarded in Germany." On behalf of the University Dahlmann stressed that all scholarship was meaningless if it did not enrich society and that scholars more than anyone else were called to preserve the sacred flame of the love of the Fatherland.

Before 1848 this dedication to an exclusive patriotism and this emphasis on the power-state were in no way characteristic of German liberals. In southwestern Germany and in the Rhineland the desire to follow western ways prevailed. The year 1819 saw the introduction of parliamentary institutions in Bavaria, Baden, and Württemberg. The leader of the liberal opposition in Baden was Karl von Rotteck who taught history and political science at the University of his native town, Freiburg. In his time his influence on the educated middle class in southern Germany was very great. His multivoluminous *Universal History* reached its 25th printing twenty-six years after his death. His *Encyclopedia of Political Science (Staatslexikon)* which he edited with his young colleague, Karl Theodor Welcker, was, in the 1830's, a powerful vehicle for spreading western liberal ideas. The Chamber of Deputies in Baden, originally modeled after that of the French Charte of 1814 became after 1831, with the growing influence of French liberalism, the first school of parliamentary life in Germany.

Rotteck's spiritual home was not the War of Liberation but the Enlightenment. The state to him was primarily the embodiment not of might, but of right. Like so many other eighteenth century Germans, he lavished no praise on great conquerors and least of all on Frederick II of Prussia. Like most German liberals of 1830 he demanded the restoration of Poland's independence. In his *History* he called the partition of Poland "the most horrible violation of international law and of the sacred right of mankind in modern times, infinitely more terrible than the horrors of the Huns and the Vandals." Rotteck believed in natural law, which the Germans called *Vernunftrecht,* rational law. He also admired the United States. "There no secret police, no censorship, no suspension of personal liberty, no closing of the borders, no terrorist measures were needed to maintain public tranquility and the respect for authority." Rotteck was neither a revolutionary nor a republican. He sought to transform Baden and southwestern Germany into a bulwark of western liberty rivaling England, France, and Belgium. "For Rotteck," writes Professor Sell, "liberty unquestionably took precedence over nationalism. In the Napoleonic period he proved himself a patriot; Napoleon as he saw it had suppressed liberty." But he was reluctant to sacrifice the liberty acquired in a small German state for the nation at large if that were less liberal. He preferred being the citizen of a constitutional free state to being the subject of a great power. After the German Festival of Hambach in 1832 he delivered a speech in Badenweiler in which he exclaimed: "I do not desire [national] unity without [political] liberty, and I prefer liberty without unity to unity without liberty. I reject unity under the wings of the Prussian or Austrian eagle." When war between liberal France and reactionary Prussia threatened to break out Rotteck was of the opinion that in such a case liberal Germany should side with France.

*   *   *

When the Prussian army under Prince William, the future William I, moved southward to suppress democracy in Germany, it found the stiffest resistance in Baden. There Lorenz Brentano, a lawyer from Mannheim, proclaimed a republic with the support of the majority of the population. The people fought well. The Swiss poet Gottfried Keller, who was then in Heidelberg and could observe the war at close range, wrote: "The Prussians paid dearly for their victory though they had superior forces. Especially the Baden artillerymen showed great heroism. As it was very hot, they worked at their guns in shirtsleeves as bakers do in front of the oven, and yet they were in high spirits. They shot their own wounded comrades to death to prevent them from falling into Prussian hands." The superior equipment and numbers of the Prussian army rendered resistance hopeless.

What the Russian troops did at about the same time in Hungary, Prussian soldiers accomplished in south-western Germany. German liberty was extinguished in a reign of terror. Nearly a thousand men were sentenced to long terms of hard labor, and over forty were executed. Out of a population of nearly one and one half million, eighty thousand citizens left Baden for Switzerland, England, and the United States. Almost equally great was the number who fled the Palatinate and the Rhineland. The revolutions of 1849 in Baden and the Palatinate were the last attempt to introduce democracy into Germany. An authoritarian exclusive nationalism triumphed in 1848 and carried Germany along a road far removed from that traced by Rotteck and Gervinus.

Before 1848 German liberals hoped to achieve both national unity and political liberty. In the nineteenth century in western Europe nationalism and democratic liberalism supported and strengthened each other. The same process took place during the century in most Germanic lands—in Switzerland, in the Netherlands, and in Scandinavia. The Germans, however, did not succeed in uniting the two forces. The great majority of them desired national power even above liberty.

There were those who hoped that liberty would come after the creation of a strong nation-state. Recalling Periclean Athens and Elizabethan England, they insisted that great civilizations flourish under a strong government. But history exhibits many examples of artistic activity under weak governments, to mention only the Italian Renaissance and the ferment of Germany in Goethe's generation. But whatever might have been the hopes and illusions of the German national liberals, they preferred nationalism, and their liberalism was short-lived. Two critical years in the surrender of liberalism were 1848 and 1866. In both cases few Germans could resist the lure of power, a power embodied in the Prussian military monarchy.

After the Revolution of 1848 in Paris fanned the hopes of democracy in central Europe, the German liberals had to choose one of two alternatives. One was to reform the governments in the various German states, to call democratic assemblies in each, and thus to replace the absolutist authorities by popular institutions. Later on, the new democratic German states could have formed, by democratic means, a closer and more perfect union. In their haste to establish national unity, the German liberals proceeded otherwise. Instead of reforming and democratizing the various individual states—as the Swiss did in their cantons after 1831—and thus laying the foundations for German democracy, they ignored local institutions, traditional seats of loyalty and power, and called a democratically elected National Assembly to Frankfurt-am-Main, an assembly which rested on no real foundations and was not supported by any existing political structure. It was an overly ambitious project. For that very reason it achieved neither liberty nor unity. During the many months that it took to work out a democratic constitution for the whole of Germany the authoritarian governments of the various German lands, which in the spring of 1848 had briefly lost control of the situation, reasserted themselves, and the democratic constitution was doomed. Unity was achieved twenty years later by a determined adversary of liberal democracy, by Bismarck.

The National Assembly went further in predetermining the course of German history. No German prince of the time stood in as sharp an opposition to all western concepts of liberty and parliamentarism as did King Frederick William IV of Prussia. When he opened, on April 11, 1847, the first session of the United Estates (*Vereinigte Landtag*) representing the various provinces of his kingdom, he warned the assembly against the un-Germanic and impractical illusion that it might be possible to realize in Germany parliamentary institutions. No power on earth, he solemnly professed, would ever succeed in making him change the natural relation between prince and people into a constitutional one. He swore that he would never allow a constitution, a piece of paper, to come between our Lord in Heaven and his (the king's) country, "to govern us with its articles and to replace old and sacred loyalties." He was convinced that his people would resist the wiles of seduction, that they did not wish to share in the government through their representatives and to break the plenitude of power entrusted by God to their kings. "I and my House, we wish to serve the Lord."

At the time this medieval approach aroused general consternation. Only Ranke was so naive as to believe that since King David no king had uttered more beautiful words. "I say definitely," he wrote, "that I know nothing since the psalms where the idea of a religious monarchy has been expressed more powerfully and more nobly. It has great passages of historical truth." Though the national liberals in Frankfurt did not share Ranke's profound devotion and put their hope instead in a liberal Prussia, they were so fascinated by Prussian power that in April, 1849, they offered the imperial crown of Germany to King Frederick William IV. The king, more faithful to his principles than the majority of liberals in the National Assembly were to theirs, rejected the crown offered to him by the democratically elected representatives of the nation. The Prussian ruling class had no faith in nation or people, in democracy or parliament. They expected the regeneration of Prussia from Prussia's traditional pillar of strength, the army. *"Gegen Demokraten helfen nur Soldaten"*—Only soldiers are of help against democrats—expressed the then prevailing mood in Berlin. After the failure of the Frankfurt Assembly to achieve German unity, many of the national liberals came to share their faith in Prussia's mission and in Prussia's army.

Before 1848 the national liberals expected Prussia to be absorbed in Germany. In an article published in the *Deutsche Zeitung* on January 1, 1848, Dahlmann pleaded for an hereditary imperial monarchy under the Hohenzollern. But he rejected the idea of Prussian domination over Germany and insisted that the German parliament must not meet in Berlin. On the contrary, he demanded, "the German Reichstag should have its seat anywhere but on Prussian soil. . . . In a short time there must be no Prussian region which has not felt the rejuvenating breath of free German life." Prussia was to be Germanized, not Germany Prussianized. There was widespread hope among the liberals that Prussia could be dissolved into its various provinces which would become in their own right part of the united Germany. Thus the threat presented to German liberty and cultural life by Prussia's overwhelming power and tradition might be averted. This seemed not impossible in 1847. Most Prussian provinces were still corporate personalities with their own traditions, their own Estates, and their own administrations. In March, 1848, a strong separatist movement made itself felt in the Prussian Rhineland.

The experience of the year 1848–49 changed the outlook of the national liberals. In a recent book, *Liberal Thought at the Time of the Frankfurt Assembly,* the young German historian Wolfgang Hock has carefully followed the progress of many German intellectuals from an initial clear distinction between national might and self-interest on the one hand and right and morality on the other, to their harmonization and identification.

Gustav Rümelin took this to be the mission which "our German people received from history," to make morality ever more political and politics ever more moral. Such an attempt at the harmonization of might and morality was facilitated by several factors: the educated German middle class lacked political experience. It had not shared in the political life of the country or in the administration of the state, which was reserved for the closed caste of professional bureaucrats. German thought had been predominantly philosophical and poetical and had neglected the realities of state and power as well as the task of responsible self-government and political education of the citizen.

Now the intellectuals seized upon the revelation of power—from the exercise of which they remained excluded—with typical German thoroughness, and with the enthusiasm of converts to a new faith. They overestimated and idealized power and the state as much as they had formerly underestimated them. They overlooked the necessary limits and inherent dangers of power. They were convinced that these dangers did not exist when power was in the right hands, in the hands of a morally superior and better educated governing class or nation. The new vision of power and national greatness was intoxicating. The danger was all the greater the more sincerely these educated Germans were convinced of their own morality and rationality. They lacked even a slight—and often healthy—dash of humor, of cynicism, or of self-criticism. They were deeply in earnest. Thus they easily succumbed to temptation without even being aware of it. Jacob Burckhardt saw this clearly. On August 23, 1848, he wrote to his German friend, Hermann Schaumburg: "Do what you wish or must do, only don't imagine that you are free while in reality the darkest elemental spirits dwell in you and drive you on (*die dunkelsten Elementargeister ihr Wesen mit Euch treiben*)."

An understandable desire for action, for a new fulness of life, animated the educated German middle class. They no longer wished to be a people of thinkers, poets, and dreamers. Impatiently they longed for great deeds on the world stage. The pettier the present appeared to them the mightier was their vision of the future. They knew that German classical literature was great. In their eyes it represented a unique re-embodiment of the heritage of Greece. But now its task was fulfilled. The time had come to assert German political leadership as Luther had three centuries before established German religious leadership. A man like Luther was needed, not in the field of religion but in the realm of politics. How could such a great destiny be realized without the help of those in power?

Dahlmann, in the speech of January 22, 1849, in which he proposed the imperial crown for Prussia, voiced the growing conviction that power was more important than liberty. "The path of power," he declared, "is the only one which can satisfy and satiate our urge for liberty. For this urge does not primarily aspire to liberty; to a greater degree it lusts for power which has so far been denied to it. This can be accomplished only through Prussia. Prussia can not thrive (genesen) without Germany nor Germany without Prussia." The same shift to a preference for state-power over liberty can be traced, as Professor Felix Gilbert has shown, in the thought of another great liberal historian, Droysen. In 1847 he had written that history teaches us everywhere that the longing for power and glory deludes nations and states, for it overstimulates and finally brutalizes and debilitates them. But at the end of 1848, in the midst of the popular uprisings, he confessed that he saw in the [Prussian] army a great moral force, and that power alone could save Germany. "The State is Power," he proclaimed as did Treitschke later. Droysen now abandoned the hope that Prussia would become Germanized and a part of Germany; on the contrary, Prussia in its full power and armed with the Prussian tradition appeared as the political savior of Germany. In a revolutionary year men and movements travel rapidly a long road, some forward to liberty, others backward to the apparent security of great power.

*   *   *

The Germans of the Age of Nationalism had no liberal statesman, no Gladstone, not even a Cavour, Clemenceau, or Masaryk, to direct their national energies into democratic channels. Instead, they had Bismarck. What the revolution of 1848 failed to do, his revolution of 1866 accomplished. It laid the foundations of a unified German nation-state. Bismarck put the Hohenzollern into the position which the Hohenstaufen once occupied. But the foundations laid by Bismarck seemed stronger at that time than they were shown to be a few decades later. Solitary voices crying in the wilderness of national self-satisfaction warned Bismarck's admirers in vain against overestimating power and underestimating liberty. For 1866 failed even more disastrously than 1848 in securing liberty and infusing nationalism with the spirit of democracy.

Dr. Neill views the alliance and conflict of liberalism and nationalism in terms of social classes.

FROM *The Rise and Decline of Liberalism*

BY THOMAS P. NEILL

IN THE FIRST HALF of the nineteenth century Liberalism was inextricably bound in with the all-pervading romanticism of the age, and outside of

Thomas P. Neill, *The Rise and Decline of Liberalism* (1953), pp. 123–30, 132. Reprinted by permission of The Bruce Publishing Company.

England and France with nationalism. Liberalism and nationalism are frequently called twin offspring of the French Revolution, twins who supported and helped each other grow in the first half of the century, but who turned against each other about 1850 with the ever stronger nationalism eventually smothering the ever weakening Liberalism. Italy is perhaps the best example of the close association, almost identification, of Liberalism and nationalism in the first part of the century. Germany and Poland are other good examples. At this time there was no geographic Italy or Germany or Poland. Italy was cut up into a number of states, some under foreign and others under native control. Nationalists who wanted to create a united Italy therefore instinctively embraced Liberal doctrines as excellent weapons to turn against the existing authorities. So it was with Germans who were divided among thirty-nine states, or Poles who lived under the rule of Prussia, Austria, and Russia.

In each of these areas the nationalists imported Liberal theory from abroad, and though it served their revolutionary purpose, it was an abstract kind of thought not associated with their national traditions or their various histories. When a national state was finally created in Italy in 1861 and in Germany a decade later, it was therefore easy for the new governments to suppress Liberalism as annoying and as dangerous to the established government. Thus Liberalism tended to lose out to nationalism in the latter part of the century, but it did not disappear without leaving its mark on each country, and in many countries it continued as the program of a minority group. As an opposition party in Germany, for example, the Liberals kept their theory alive and pushed upon Bismarck a number of measures he might otherwise never have adopted. So it was in Italy, in Spain, in Portugal, and in other countries where Liberalism tended to disappear as a doctrine or as a party label.

Liberalism failed to take root in the countries outside France, we have suggested, principally because there was no large middle class anywhere else in Europe in the early nineteenth century. And the middle class is the good ground in which the seed of Liberal doctrine takes root and grows. It is worth noting in this connection that Liberalism spread chiefly in the Rhineland, in Belgium and Holland, in northern Italy, and in other local areas where there was a numerous middle class. But nowhere outside England, France, Holland, and Belgium were the bourgeoisie numerous or influential enough to control the nation as a whole. The Rhinelanders, for example, were in a Prussia dominated by the *Junkertum* of the East, and the bourgeoisie of northern Italy had to contend with the central and southern provinces as well as opponents in their own area. It is this lack of a large middle class, more than any other single factor, which explains the failure of Liberalism in such countries as Hungary and Poland, where the political and social situation seemed otherwise ideally cast for the triumph of Liberalism.

The near success and the ultimate failure of Liberalism in Germany is more important for the subsequent history of the movement than its fate anywhere else in central or southern Europe. It should be remembered that the western and southern parts of the German-speaking world had been within the orbit of French influence throughout the eighteenth century, that the Liberal ideas of such writers as Montesquieu and Voltaire and Rousseau and of such groups as the Encyclopedists and Physiocrats were well known in these parts of Germany. This thought developed into a German brand of the Enlightenment, known as the *Aufklärung,* which prepared the way intellectually for the advance of Liberalism in the early nineteenth century.

The first Liberal victories, paradoxically, were not won by Liberals but were imposed on Prussians by their government. These were the Liberal reforms of Hardenberg and vom Stein, a part of that larger movement in Prussian history early in the nineteenth century when the country of Frederick the Great came to life again after its humiliations at Napoleon's hands. The Prussian government had watched Napoleon's conscript army, fired by a burning nationalism and an intense love of liberty, tear their professional army to pieces time and time again. After Prussia's worst humiliations of all, the defeats of Jena and Auerstadt and the partitioning of the country at Tilsit in 1807, the ministry set about reviving the country and readying it for a "war of liberation" against Napoleon.

Military reform under men like Gneisenau and Scharnhorst was of a liberal character. Social and political and economic reforms were likewise liberal, enough so at any rate to satisfy the modest requests of Rhineland Liberals and to serve as the springboard for future Liberal demands for constitutional government and a bill of rights. Vom Stein and Hardenberg, leaders in the Prussian revival after 1807, wanted to destroy the relics of feudalism so as to set up a society of free men, partly because the French experience proved free men better soldiers and partly because men like vom Stein and Hardenberg were influenced by the *Aufklärung.* A series of land reforms under vom Stein ended serfdom and threw the ownership of land open to all classes in Prussia. At the same time freedom of occupation was asserted for all citizens.

The most important Liberal change in politics was the setting up of a system of local self-government which, it should be noted, was widely interpreted as the first step toward constitutional government on the English model. Thus Ruggiero has written:

> The projects of Hardenberg [and vom Stein] were permeated by this spirit of freedom. He demanded so much liberty and equality as was compatible with monarchy and a free civil society: the abolition of the privileges of the nobility with regard to public office, possession of baronial lands, and exemption from taxes: the abolition of the hereditary dependence of the peasants and the restrictions on the acquisition and use of land: and the institution of national representation so far as this did not prejudice the principle of monarchy.

Thus it seemed a good beginning was made toward the triumph of Liberalism in Prussia by the time Napoleon was sent off to St. Helena in 1815. Moreover, the great German thinkers of this age seemed favorably disposed toward the development of a full Liberalism; the professional classes were inclined toward Liberal doctrine; and the universities, the freest and most advanced in Europe, promised to be seedbeds of future Liberal thought. However, the destinies of Germany did not lie in such persons' hands, but rather in the ruling classes', especially in Austria and Prussia. The governments of these two states proved abnormally fearful of all Liberal thought. Metternich believed that Liberalism would dissolve his world. His mission was to preserve that world as long as he was in power, and until 1848 he controlled German destinies through the Confederation set up at Vienna after Napoleon's defeat.

Liberalism was realized in a modified way, however, in some of the smaller states, especially those in the southwest, where new constitutions were adopted on the model of the French *Charte* of 1814. Baden and Bavaria received such constitutions in 1818, Württemberg adopted one in 1819, and after the disturbances of 1830 Saxony and Hanover adopted moderately Liberal constitutions. Until the Revolution of 1848 Liberalism achieved no other notable victories in the German Confederation. Prussia unintentionally promoted the growth of the middle class, and indirectly therefore of Liberalism, by following a vigorous free trade policy throughout these years. Such a policy derived from political necessity rather than Liberal theory, for the Prussian government found that it could not enforce tariff duties in a state with such long, broken, and irregular borders as it had after 1815. It therefore followed a policy of free trade with neighboring states, and eventually by 1834 created the famous *Zollverein* or Customs Union of German states clustering in a free trade area around Prussia. This measure, together with a few minor enactments, such as a law of 1838 encouraging the construction of railroads, or the Prussian Code of Labor of 1845 based on freedom of contract for workers, promoted the growth of the middle class in Prussia and to some extent in neighboring German states.

The growth of a commercial and industrial class in Germany after 1815 was of course helpful for the development of Liberalism. Until about 1830 German Liberals were generally writers, students, and professors; after that date more and more commercial and industrial leaders appear in the Liberal camp, men such as David Hansemann, a merchant of Aachen, and Ludwig Camphausen, Liberal Prussian statesman of 1848. Industrialism had not developed sufficiently by 1848, however, to produce a class in Germany such as existed in England two decades earlier, a class capable of taking over the revolution of that year and directing it along practical Liberal lines. Control was exercised instead by the professors, who at mid-century were still the dominant Liberal class in Germany.

It is customary to divide German Liberalism of this period into radical and moderate camps, with the radicals found mostly in the southern states and the moderates found chiefly in the Rhineland. For our purposes it is sufficient to note that all Liberals came to agree on this program: they must liberate the German states from the paternalism of Austria and the influence of Metternich; they must obtain genuinely Liberal constitutions for all these states, especially for Prussia, which must lead the Liberal struggle against Austria; finally, they must join these states together into a united German state. Thus the Liberals found themselves tied in with the national movement to create a united German state.

These Liberals differed from other nationalists chiefly in their insistence on the rights and liberties of German citizens, which for them were as important as the goal of German unity. Carl Rotteck, called "a typical representative of unhistorical, doctrinaire Liberalism," modeled his thought closely on that of Royer-Collard. Rotteck based human rights on abstract reason rather than on historical precedent. In a fashion strongly similar to the French Doctrinaires he drew up plans for ideal constitutional government and formulated a set of guarantees to preserve such government from royal tyranny or mob despotism. Liberals such as Rotteck conspired in romantic fashion to seize the reins of government and to unify the German states whenever the opportunity should present itself. Several times in the thirty years after 1815 they thought the time for such revolutionary Liberalism had come, but it was not until 1848 that they had a real chance to direct their nation's destiny.

In that year of universal revolution the Liberals had an opportunity to take over every government on the Continent—and for a few months it seemed that they would succeed everywhere. German revolutionary activity began toward the end of February in Baden, where Liberal agitators demonstrated and Liberal politicians came to power without violence or bloodshed. Similar spontaneous upheavals occurred at once in Bavaria and other southwestern German states. Within a few weeks the governments of other such states as Hanover and Saxony had fallen and the Liberals were in control. Early in March demonstrations began in the streets of Vienna. Metternich was forced to resign and flee to England. A new ministry made the typical Liberal promises to satisfy the urban-manned insurrection: the Imperial Estates would be summoned to draw up a constitution; censorship would be abolished; a bourgeois national guard would be organized. In Berlin the Prussian king capitulated to a demonstrating crowd, appointed a more liberal ministry, and called for elections to a constituent assembly.

Thus by the end of March, 1848, Liberalism seemed triumphant throughout the thirty-nine German states. Constitutions were being made according to Liberal theory. The old regime had collapsed everywhere, and it only remained for the new Liberal governments to consolidate their position and to create a Liberal national German state. To accomplish this latter important task Liberal leaders had summoned a parliament to meet at

Frankfurt in May. For a time all went well in this "professors' parliament." There was much heated debate on a bill of rights and on the form of government best suited for Liberal society. Eventually the new constitution was finished, and the smaller states were generally in favor of adopting it. But meanwhile the anti-Liberal leaders of Prussia and Austria had recovered their positions and had come back to rule in Berlin and Vienna. Their refusal to accept the Liberal national constitution of Frankfurt, together with the inability of the "professors" parliament to force its solution on the two major states, spelled the ruin of Liberalism throughout the Germanies.

Liberalism had failed to stay in power for a number of reasons. It had taken hold only in the cities, which in Germany did not contain a sizable proportion of the population. When the revolution spread out into the countryside, therefore, urban Liberalism was swamped under rural conservatism. Liberalism, moreover, had taken root only in the middle class, and in Germany this was not a sufficiently strong or large class to govern by itself. The movement did not receive active support from peasant, artisan, or aristocratic elements in the nation. Finally, Liberal leadership was incredibly inefficient. It achieved its initial successes only because the existing governments had been caught off guard by spontaneous demonstrations in the various capitals. When Liberals found themselves in power, however, they were unprepared to rule. The "professors' parliament" characteristically talked long about fundamental rights when they should have been solving the more pressing problem of what to do with Austria and Prussia in the proposed national state.

* * *

Perhaps the Frankfurt Assembly was too much interested in getting a constitution on paper and formulating a full declaration of rights, and not enough concerned with practical problems of government. Whatever the causes—and the story of 1848 is a very confused and complex one—the Liberals failed to stem the tide of reaction under the old professional ruling classes. Their failure meant the failure of Liberalism as a political philosophy and a system of government. "The example of Frankfurt, aggravated by the historians' misrepresentations, was fatal to German political Liberalism. The people lost all interest in representative institutions, and made up its mind, to its own loss, that its political future depended wholly upon the Crown. The tradition of a paternal state was too strong, especially in Prussia, for a single assembly of Liberals to destroy it with a declaration of fundamental rights and liberties of the German citizen. Nationalism remained the more pressing issue after 1848. The Liberals had failed to create a national state when they had their chance. The next opportunity was to fall to Bismarck, who, disgusted by the professorial verbiage at Frankfurt, decided that unification was to be accomplished not by words but by blood and iron.

*Professor Hayes of Columbia University was a life-long stu-
dent of nationalism. In the following essay he sums up what
he considers to be the inevitable result of the clash of liberalism and nationalism, particularly in cases similar to that of
Germany.*

FROM *Essays on Nationalism*

BY CARLTON J. H. HAYES

LET US SUPPOSE that a nationality has waged several wars of self-
determination and finally established a sovereign national state. Let us suppose, further, that this state has been successful in irredentist struggles and
has acquired every bit of territory inhabited by any considerable number of
fellow nationals. Let us concede that the wars of national self-determination
were of the nature of enthusiastic popular rebellions against intolerable
abuses of alien tyranny and that they evoked from the rebels the noblest
idealism and the most heroic deeds. Let us concede, too, even in respect of
the subsequent irredentist conflicts, that they were precipitated by muddling
attempts of a corrupt empire to restrict the liberties of its dissident nationalities and that they represent an honest and just effort to "redeem" a population, the large majority of whom truly yearned to become citizens of the
emancipating national state. It is reasonable to infer from the circumstances
that "liberals" and "radicals" and "humanitarians" and "progressives" in all
countries acclaimed with one voice the spiritual grandeur of that nationality,
that the wealthier among them contributed to relief funds in aid of its
wounded and destitute and subscribed to the war-bonds of its government,
and that the more romantic volunteered their lives in its military service and
their pens in its journalistic propaganda.

We might imagine, if we knew no history and were incorrigible opti-
mists, that such a nationality, that such a national state, would thenceforth be
an exemplar of justice and charity to all other nationalities and national
states and a pillar of world-peace. Unfortunately, however, the history of the
nineteenth and twentieth centuries, whilst it gives ample support to our
suppositions concerning the altruism and lofty purpose of wars of national
self-determination and even of irredentist wars, affords little or no evidence
that the attainment of national independence and unity is a sure preliminary

Carlton J. H. Hayes, *Essays on Nationalism* (1926), pp. 156–9. Reprinted by permission of
Evelyn Carroll Hayes.

to international peace and brotherhood. On the contrary, it bears witness to the disquieting fact that nationalism does not exhaust its functions and resources when it unites a dismembered nationality and erects a national state; it shows that almost invariably nationalism is heightened rather than lessened by the attainment of national sovereignty and that a national state, so soon as it is solidly established, proceeds to evolve a "national policy," which is as bellicose as it is nationalist.

What this "national policy" is, has been nicely indicated in an illuminating essay by Mr. J. L. Stocks: ". . . the 'national' policy of an established State . . . means, of course, a policy of national selfishness and aggrandisement, a 'sacred egoism,' made sacred, presumably, by the sentiment of nationality. Internally its effort is to strengthen and tighten the national bond by every means in its power; externally to make the nation feared or 'respected' by a bold and firm foreign policy, backed by a sufficiency of military force, and to obtain for it a share in the riches of the undeveloped portions of the earth's surface. It appeals to the cruder forms of patriotism. Its love of country turns readily into hatred of the foreigner, its desire for prosperity into competition for territory; and the duty of service is interpreted as a duty to maintain national unity by unquestioning assent to every decision of government. The appropriate political ideas are instilled into the citizen by the machinery of public education and by compulsory military service; and direct inducement not to surrender these ideas in later life is easily supplied if the state keeps control over appointments in some of the main professions, especially the teaching profession, and is liberal in its rewards to right-thinking leaders of opinion. Such a policy is necessarily the antithesis of nineteenth-century liberalism. In the interest of national unity it will ruthlessly suppress dissentient groups within the nation, and will be prepared for whatever sacrifice may be necessary of the principle of free speech and thought. It will develop a national economy with all its machinery of tariffs, subsidies, and concessions. In every sphere it will tend to penalise the foreigner, in its colonies by frank preference for the trade and capital of the home country, at home by interposing obstacles to immigration and naturalisation. The rulers of Germany perceived further that a certain measure of what is called State Socialism is of assistance to the objects of this policy, which are to make nationality overwhelmingly important to the citizen and so strengthen the hands of government."

In other words, an established national state evolves, under nationalism, "national interests" at home and abroad; its citizens similarly develop "national rights," more national rights perhaps when they are abroad than when they are at home; and, above all, the aggregate of national state and its citizens come to possess a peculiarly precious "national honour." Now, to assure national interests and national rights and to preserve national honour, an established state, even more than a would-be nation, must be prepared to use force and to wage war. Militarism thus becomes an abiding characteristic of nationalism and the chief means to nationalist ends. Militarism is not merely a temporary instrument thrust by a fortuitous Providence into the hands of oppressed nationalities and idyllic irredentists and enabling them to recast political geography on reasonable national lines. Militarism, with its displays of might and threats of force, is a permanent feature of triumphant nationalism in a world in which non-national empires have largely been replaced by national states.

EDITED BY

Brian Tierney,
Donald Kagan &
L. Pearce Williams
CORNELL UNIVERSITY

RANDOM HOUSE HISTORICAL ISSUES SERIES